REGULAR SINGING

Conversations on November 22nd, 2011
The Fiftieth Anniversary of
the Assassination of President John F Kennedy

Play 4
The Apple Family
Scenes from Life in the Country

Richard Nelson

BROADWAY PLAY PUBLISHING INC
New York
BroadwayPlayPub.com

REGULAR SINGING
© Copyright 2014 by Richard Nelson

First printing: February 2014
Second printing: December 2014

I S B N: 978-0-88145-588-5

Book design: Marie Donovan
Page make-up: Adobe Indesign
Typeface: Palatino
Printed and bound in the U S A

PLAYS BY RICHARD NELSON

Artists In America:
FRANK'S HOME*
FAREWELL TO THE THEATRE
NIKOLAI AND THE OTHERS
THE PECULIAR NATURE OF CITIES
(scheduled for production)

Plays of Adolescence, A Trilogy:
GOODNIGHT CHILDREN EVERYWHERE
FRANNY'S WAY*
MADAME MELVILLE

England/America, A Special Relationship:
SOME AMERICANS ABROAD
TWO SHAKESPEAREAN ACTORS
NEW ENGLAND
WHERE I COME FROM

American History Plays:
COLUMBUS AND THE DISCOVERY OF JAPAN
THE GENERAL FROM AMERICA
HOW SHAKESPEARE WON THE WEST*
CONVERSATIONS IN TUSCULUM

The Apple Family Plays:
Part One: THAT HOPEY CHANGEY THING*
Part Two: SWEET AND SAD*
Part Three: SORRY*
Part Four: REGULAR SINGING*

Other Plays:
BETWEEN EAST AND WEST*
PRINICIPIA SCRIPTORIAE
ROOTS IN WATER*
RODNEY'S WIFE*
MISHA'S PARTY *(with Alexander Gelman)*
LEFT*
KENNETH'S FIRST PLAY* *(with Colin Chambers)*

Early Plays:
THE KILLING OF YABLONSKI*
SCOOPING*
CONJURING AN EVENT*
JUNGLE COUP*
THE VIENNA NOTES*
BAL*
THE RETURN OF PINOCCHIO*
RIP VAN WINKLE OR 'THE WORKS'*
AN AMERICAN COMEDY*

Musicals:
UNFINISHED PIECE FOR A PLAYER PIANO
(with Peter Golub)
PARADISE FOUND
(with Ellen Fitzhugh & Jonathan Tunick)
MY LIFE WITH ALBERTINE *(with Ricky Ian Gordon)*
JAMES JOYCE'S THE DEAD *(with Shaun Davey)*
CHESS
(with Tim Rice, Benny Andersson, Björn Ulvaeus)

Translations:
Gogol: THE INSPECTOR
(with Richard Pevear & Larissa Volokhonsky)
Turgenev: A MONTH IN THE COUNTRY
(with Richard Pevear & Larissa Volokhonsky)
Bulgakov: DON QUIXOTE
(with Richard Pevear & Larissa Volokhonsky)
Ibsen: THE WILD DUCK*, ENEMY OF THE PEOPLE
(Also adaptation)*
Strindberg: MISS JULIE*, THE FATHER*
Molière: DON JUAN*
Goldoni: IL CAMPIELLO*
Pirandello: ENRICO IV*
Erdman: THE SUICIDE*
Brecht: JUNGLE OF CITIES, THE WEDDING
Chekhov: THE SEAGULL*, THE CHERRY ORCHARD*,
THREE SISTERS*, THE WOOD DEMON*
Fo: ACCIDENTAL DEATH OF AN ANARCHIST
Carriere: THE CONTROVERSY AT VALLADOID

Adaptations:
TYNAN *(with Colin Chambers)*
from the Diaries of Kenneth Tynan
LOLITA, *edited for the stage, from the novel by Nabokov*
JITTERBUGGING*
adapted from Schnitzler's LA RONDE

*Published by Broadway Play Publishing Inc

REGULAR SINGING was commissioned by The Public Theater (Oskar Eustis, Artistic Director; Patrick Willingham, Executive Director). The play opened at the Public Theater on 22 November 2013. The cast and creative contributors were:

RICHARD..Jay O Sanders
BARBARA .... Maryann Plunkett
MARIAN...Laila Robins
JANE .... Sally Murphy
BENJAMIN ....Jon DeVries
TIM .... Stephen Kunken

Director.. Richard Nelson
Scenic & costume design ....Susan Hilferty
Lighting design ....Jennifer Tipton
Sound design............................ Scott Lehrer & Will Pickens
Production stage manager ....Pamela Salling
Stage manager.. Maggie Swing
Assistant director... Tamara Frisch
Production assistant .... Caroline Englander
Prop masters ..... Rebecca David, Amelia Freeman-Lynde
Prop runcrew ....Lily Perlmutter
Intern .... Luke Anderson

CHARACTERS & SETTING

The APPLES:

RICHARD APPLE, *a lawyer in the Governor's office, now lives in Albany.*

BARBARA APPLE, *his sister, a high school English teacher, lives in Rhinebeck*

MARIAN APPLE, *his sister, a third-grade teacher. Lives in Rhinebeck.*

JANE APPLE, *his sister, a non-fiction writer, lives in Rhinebeck with her boyfriend,* Tim.

BENJAMIN APPLE, *his uncle, a retired actor, lives in an assisted living home, in Beacon, NY.*

TIM ANDREWS, *actor, lives in Rhinebeck with* JANE APPLE.

The play takes place between approximately 10 P M and a little after midnight of Friday, November 22ⁿᵈ, 2013.

Rhinebeck, New York; a small historic village one hundred miles north of New York City; once referred to in an article in The New York Times *as "The Town That Time Forgot". A room in* BARBARA APPLE'*s house, on Center Street, which she shares with* MARIAN, *and, for the last month, with* MARIAN'*s ex-husband, Adam Platt.*

SUMMARY

Play one: THAT HOPEY CHANGEY THING is set on Nov. 2, 2010. Before the play begins, Uncle Benjamin Apple, a well-known actor, has had a heart attack, which sent him into a coma. When he came out of the coma, he had serious amnesia. By the beginning of the play, he has retired, and moved into his niece Barbara's home in Rhinebeck, New York.

Play two: SWEET AND SAD is set on Sept. 11, 2011. Months before the play begins, Marian's twenty-year-old daughter, Evan, committed suicide, for reasons unknown. Since then, Marian and her husband, Adam, have separated, and Marian now shares Barbara's house with Barbara and Benjamin.

Play three: SORRY is set on Nov. 6, 2012. Richard has been on a lengthy business trip to England; Barbara and Marian have been waiting for his return before moving Benjamin to an assisted living home. A move which Barbara has been resisting. Marian continues to share Barbara's house with Barbara and Benjamin.

"For a long time I would go to bed early."
—opening of *Swann's Way*

for
Cynthia, Marian, Bill, Jim & Rob

(*A wooden table and four wooden chairs. A few short-stemmed mostly dead flowers in a small glass bowl on the table. Rugs.*)

(*Animal Collective's* My Girls *begins;* BARBARA *enters with a tablecloth that she begins to put on the table, and with a small bouquet of colorful flowers, with which she will replace the mostly dead flowers in the glass bowl. The flowers are a burst of color in the room.*)

(MARIAN *soon follows with a tray of various dishes, bowls, casserole dishes covered in foil—the remnants of a pot luck supper—chicken salad, pasta, bean salad, homemade fries, green salad, little hot dogs, etc. The bowls, dishes, etc—have taped labels, and totally unmatched, coming as they do from various households.*)

(JANE *soon carries in a tray of used paper plates, plastic glasses, used napkins, used silverware, etc.*)

(JANE *and* MARIAN *will go off and return a few times, bringing in more dishes and bottles of wine and soda, and a bottle of Irish Whiskey.*)

(BARBARA *will go off and return with a card table, which she sets up and on which most of the drinks will be set, as "the bar".*)

(RICHARD *and* TIM *enter with chairs; they make a number of trips and bring in numerous chairs—perhaps as many as twelve or fourteen—which they set around the room, against the "walls" —in small groupings where the recent guests had gathered themselves.*)

(All set the used paper plates, plastic glasses and cups, and the used napkins around the room—on the floor, under chairs, on empty chairs where the guests recently were, so that a picture finally emerges of a just finished pot luck dinner for ten or so guests.)

(BENJAMIN joins RICHARD and TIM; as the women leave, the men sit…)

(It is ten at night on November 22, 2013.)

Gentlemen Singing

(BENJAMIN, RICHARD and TIM. TIM has some Xeroxed sheet music; BENJAMIN sits at a distance, he looks around the room. TIM sings [from the Ainsworth Psalter, Psalm 13] to RICHARD.)

TIM: *(Singing)*
How long Jehovah, wilt thou me forget for aye:
How long-while wilt thou hide thy face from me
 away?
(Then) Listen to this… *(Sings)*
How long shall in my soul, my counsels set dayly
Sad sorrow in my heart, how long shall my foe be
Exalted over me?
(Then) Why would he choose that?

RICHARD: I'm surprised. Adam wasn't even religious. Isn't. Isn't religious.

TIM: You don't have to be religious. It is beautiful. And anyway, how do we know? It's what he wanted. He picked them out. He's organized the whole—service…

RICHARD: *(Reads)* "How long shall my foe be exalted over me?" Maybe he's thinking—John Boehner? *(Smiles)* So maybe it's just political, Benjamin. That makes sense for Adam.

TIM: *(To BENJAMIN)* Are you all right? Tired?

BENJAMIN: I'm not tired, Tim. I'm all right.

TIM: *(To* RICHARD*)* He said, they're the very first songs ever sung in America.

RICHARD: *(Corrects)* By white people.

TIM: Adam told me this story: a lot of early American Puritan congregations, they only knew how to sing a handful of tunes? And they couldn't even sing those well. A leader had to sing and the rest would copy him. Line by line. *Line by line.* Adam said—some people wanted to change this, they wanted there to be written-down agreed-upon notes—so that everyone could follow at the same time and sing together. But that got other people incensed: "We need a leader. It will be the end of authority." So, Adam said, all hell broke loose. They even called it a "singing war".

RICHARD: A singing war?

TIM: In the 1720s. In America. You hungry, Benjamin?

BENJAMIN: No.

TIM: *(To* RICHARD*)* Just to agree to have notes so people could fucking sing together. A war. Then, after telling me this, Adam looks up from his sick bed, and says— "Nothing's changed. America, Tim…"

(JANE *enters from the kitchen.)*

JANE: They're *almost* all gone. Just Adam's "baby" sister… Why does she keep calling herself that?

TIM: I don't know.

RICHARD: *(Standing)* I have to go, Jane.

JANE: *(To* TIM*)* She's— *(Big. Then)* The sister's on the porch still talking to Barbara. Barbara got her that far. The mother's upstairs?

TIM: At the bedside. With Marian.

JANE: Marian okay?

(No response)

JANE: I'm going to the apartment and change. Get out of these... *(She starts to go.)*

TIM: We're staying?

JANE: I think we should, don't you? I haven't eaten. Have any of us eaten? There's a ton of food left... There's even more in the kitchen.

(TIM *"looks" at his watch.)*

TIM: Jane...

JANE: *(About staying, her reasons)* Karen's at Tina's. I've been in Albany all week. I've hardly spent any time with Marian... It's the right thing. *(She goes back out through the kitchen.)*

TIM: *(As she leaves)* They could just call... If we're needed... *(To* RICHARD*)* We're just down the street.

(RICHARD *sits back down.)*

RICHARD: I haven't seen your apartment. Nice place?

TIM: *(Continues to look through the music)* Okay. Two bedrooms. Karen likes her room. Thank you God. For an eleven-year old I suppose that's everything

(BENJAMIN *picks up the bottle of whiskey.)*

TIM: Not the whiskey, Benjamin. Please. You know that's not good for you.

(BENJAMIN *pours a glass of whiskey.)*

(TIM *just shakes his head:)*

TIM: Your sisters will blame me...

RICHARD: Why would they blame you?

TIM: *(Another Psalm:)* Adam wants us all to sing this one...

BENJAMIN: Who were all these people, Tim?

TIM: They came to see Adam. Marian's ex-husband. He's upstairs.

BENJAMIN: Some of them were laughing. And some of them were crying…

(Then)

TIM: You're going to sing with us too. Adam wants that.

BENJAMIN: Am I?

RICHARD: *(Same time)* He is?

TIM: *(To* BENJAMIN*)* Let's show, Richard. Sing with me now, Benjamin. Show him what we've been practicing… Come on. You seem very restless…

BENJAMIN: Do I? I don't feel restless. *(He joins the men.)*

TIM: Here. Here's one we've practiced.

RICHARD: You remember the songs?

BENJAMIN: I remember the songs…

TIM: The music. This one makes sense for Adam…
(23rd Psalm. Sings)
Yea though in valley of death's shade
I walk—

(After a glance at BENJAMIN, TIM *continues with* BENJAMIN*:)*

BENJAMIN & TIM: —none ill I'll fear,
Because thou art with me, thy rod,
And staff my comfort are.

(Lights fade.)

Richard Stays for Potluck.

(The same a short while later)

RICHARD: *(Sees her coming in)* Barbara… *(He stands.)*

BARBARA: *(Entering)* I'm going to get out of these. *(Her shoes)* …Put on some slippers… *(To* RICHARD*)* I'm glad you're still here, Richard. Marian thought you'd leave right away.

RICHARD: I've been waiting. I should get back.

BARBARA: She thought you'd 'creep away into the night.'

RICHARD: *(To* TIM*)* Why would I "creep—"?

BARBARA: *(Over this, to* BENJAMIN*)* Have you eaten anything, Benjamin? You should.

BENJAMIN: I'm not hungry.

BARBARA: *(To* BENJAMIN*)* I haven't eaten. I don't think I've seen you eat anything all day.

TIM: Jane wants to have supper…

BARBARA: Richard—?

RICHARD: It's after ten. I have to go.

BARBARA: I just want to change my shoes…

RICHARD: I do have to go soon, Barbara. I was just waiting…I'm sorry…

BARBARA: You're not staying for supper?

RICHARD: *(Smiling)* I think I just said that. No.

BARBARA: He's not going to stay, Benjamin.

RICHARD: *(Stopping her)* Barbara, it's after ten o'clock at night. I'm not hungry. And if I'm going to come back tomorrow—

BARBARA: "If"?! Oh forget it, Richard. Just forget it—
(Turns to go.)

RICHARD: I'm coming back.

(BARBARA *stops.*)

RICHARD: Barbara. I just meant— *("Looks" at his watch)* It's late. *(To* TIM:*)* Isn't it?

(TIM *looks away.*)

RICHARD: Tim doesn't want to stay either.

TIM: I didn't say that.

BARBARA: *(Over this)* Go ahead, run away. You're always now running away from us. What are you so scared of? What do you think we'll do to you?

RICHARD: What are you talking about?

BARBARA: *(To* "BENJAMIN"*)* Or hiding from us now. Like a—little scamp.

RICHARD: I don't know what that means.

BARBARA: Or worse. That's Richard, your nephew, Uncle. Do you even remember him?

BENJAMIN: Richard…

RICHARD: *(Over this)* He knows who I am.

BARBARA: *(To* BENJAMIN*)* He hasn't seen you for a very long time. He's been hiding from us. *(Pointed)* I thought maybe he'd forgotten you.

BENJAMIN: *(To* RICHARD*)* I know who you are.

BARBARA: *(Over this)* I'm going to change. Benjamin, are you all right? Do you need anything? *(To* TIM*)* Is Marian, still upstairs?

(TIM *nods.*)

TIM: And his mother…

(Then notices:)

BARBARA: *(To* BENJAMIN*)* Is that whiskey? Come on now, Tim…

TIM: *(To* BARBARA*)* Some jackass brought whiskey…

BARBARA: *(To* BENJAMIN*)* Benjamin, you know better…
(To TIM*)* You both know better. *(To* RICHARD*)* Why
don't you stay the night? We'll make room.

RICHARD: There's no room, Barbara—

BARBARA: *(Over this)* We'll make room.

RICHARD: I can't.

BARBARA: Then at least stay for supper.

RICHARD: Barbara, I said—

BARBARA: It's a simple question. Requiring a simple
answer. Or do we have to beg you now, Richard?

RICHARD: You don't have to "beg" me. *(Then)* I'll stay
for supper. If it means that much to—

BARBARA: Good. Marian will appreciate that. *(She starts
to go, stops:)* Are you sure? I don't want you to feel
pressured. Like you—have to. *(As she goes, gestures at
the table:)* It's just potluck…

TIM: *(Beginning to stand)* Maybe we should pick up
some of this?

RICHARD: Let my sisters do that. *(Then)* They live—to
pick up stuff.

*(*TIM *doesn't know what to do, he sits back down. Then)*

RICHARD: Benjamin, don't tell my sisters I said that.

(Lights fade.)

Albany

(A short time later. BENJAMIN, RICHARD, *and* TIM.*)*

*(*JANE *has just returned, in comfortable clothes now.)*

JANE: I better pick up.

RICHARD: *(To* TIM*)* What did I tell you?

JANE: What are you two talking about?

TIM: Albany.

JANE: You look guilty.

TIM: I'm not— *(To* RICHARD*)* I've never even been to Albany.

JANE: *(As she picks up)* Karen and Tina are watching some movie on my computer.

TIM: They're in our apartment? What movie?

JANE: I don't know. Tina's dad, they said, was hogging theirs, so… *(Then)* They're fine, Tim. Tina's Mom keeps coming upstairs and "dropping by", they said. She's driving them crazy.

TIM: *(To* JANE*)* Good. Good for her. *(To* RICHARD*)* They're eleven-years old.

RICHARD: I'm now going to stay for supper.

JANE: So she guilt-ed you, Richard.

RICHARD: That's not the reason.

JANE: *(To* TIM*)* Karen's cold is a lot better than it was a week ago.

TIM: She missed school on Monday.

JANE: You told me on the phone. And it's like she grew another inch in a week. *(Smiles)* I've only been gone a week—

TIM: It's the lipstick.

JANE: I'm surprised you've allowed that. *(To* RICHARD*)* How long can you stay? Or should I ask Barbara? *(Smiles)*

RICHARD: She didn't "guilt" me, Jane.

JANE: *(Proving her point)* You're now staying for supper. *(Noticing)* Someone left her scarf... *(Picks it up and sets it on a chair.)* You need anything, Benjamin? You hungry?

BENJAMIN: I'm not hungry.

TIM: *(To* RICHARD*)* You had started to say something about your office.

RICHARD: About?

TIM: A young lawyer visiting...?

RICHARD: *(Remembers)* From D C. He's visiting us.

TIM: *(To* JANE*)* I asked Richard about "life in Albany".

RICHARD: And a few of us in Andrew's office, we get together and tell the young man—make sure when you meet him, ask Andrew where *he* went to law school. *(Smiles)*

TIM: What?

RICHARD: We want the kid to think this would only be polite. This kid went to Harvard. But we all know where Andrew went.

TIM: Where?

JANE: He told me this.

RICHARD: *Albany. Albany Law.* Not exactly Harvard. Or— *(His alma mater])* Columbia. *(Smiles)* The kid doesn't know this. So we're hoping he'll innocently ask. And we'll get to see— "it".

TIM: What's— "it"?

RICHARD: The— "expression" Andrew Cuomo gets when you know he's about to reach down someone's throat with his bare hands and pull out a beating heart. *(Laughs)* That expression. We hardly see it anymore. He really keeps it hidden now. He really wants to be President.

(As JANE *heads into the kitchen with the garbage:)*

JANE: You should eat something, Uncle. *I'm* hungry...

TIM: What happened when this kid—?

RICHARD: He didn't. The kid didn't. He chickened out. He's smarter than we thought.

(First BARBARA *and then* MARIAN *enter from upstairs.* BARBARA *in slippers and sweater now.* MARIAN *hasn't changed.)*

TIM: Jane's back. She's in the kitchen.

BARBARA: *(Going to the table)* Let's see what our choices are, Marian...

RICHARD: *(To* MARIAN*)* Everything all right upstairs?

MARIAN: *(That was a dumb thing to say)* No.

RICHARD: I meant, Marian...

MARIAN: Adam's sort of sleeping. *(Then To* RICHARD*)* He's dying.

RICHARD: I know.

MARIAN: I told Adam's Mom I'd bring her up some food. And Nadine... Let's see—what do we think a Jamaican will like of this...? His mother seems to eat anything...

(They watch her.)

MARIAN: That was nice... I don't think he recognized anyone, but they got to see him. Look at all this food...

(BARBARA nods, then:)

BARBARA: Chicken. Chicken's always good.

(MARIAN starts to fill a paper plate.)

BARBARA: *(Over the various bowls, to* MARIAN*)* On some of these, they didn't write their names, Marian...

MARIAN: I think I know who brought what.

TIM: *(To say something)* I've been asking Richard about 'life in Albany'.

BARBARA: I'd like to hear all about his 'Albany life'…

RICHARD: *(To* TIM*)* Andrew's giving himself a birthday party in a couple weeks. Fifty thousand dollars a ticket.

TIM: Jesus.

RICHARD: Maybe Sandra Lee is cooking and so it'll be worth it… *(Another thought)* Do we really need more casinos?

BARBARA: *(Still looking at the bowls, etc.)* Marian, look at this — they're hoping we scrub that off for them…

MARIAN: *(After a quick glance)* I know who that is.

*(*JANE *enters with plates.)*

JANE: I thought we deserved real plates. Is that okay, Barbara? *(Nodding to the scarf)* Someone left a scarf…

*(*BARBARA *goes to look at it.)*

BARBARA: And real glasses too. I hate these plastic things. *(About the scarf)* I think it's the Mom's. I'll take it upstairs… *(She sets it aside.)* I'll get glasses…

JANE: *(Calls)* And napkins. Real silverware!

MARIAN: *(To* JANE, *about the plate)* For Helen. And Nadine. We hope she eats chicken.

JANE: Nadine? You should give her a real plate.

MARIAN: I've already…

JANE: Here I'll hold this…

(They begin to transfer the food onto a real plate.)

JANE: I thought you said Nadine brought her own food? *(Then)* What if she came down and saw *us* with real plates? She'd get the totally wrong idea about us. *(Then)* What else? You said the Mom eats anything…

MARIAN: So, tell us all about Albany, Richard…

RICHARD: Marian, I hadn't realized how much Andrew and Albany are like this... (*Holds his fingers together— they are very tight.*) I hadn't realized that before I moved there. Before living there. That penny just hadn't dropped. You have to live there...

MARIAN: You going to sit there, Uncle?

BENJAMIN: Where do you want me to sit?

MARIAN: It's fine.

JANE: Should we put some of these chairs back in the other rooms?

MARIAN: Quite a few people said they wanted to come back tomorrow...

JANE: I thought you were against that.

MARIAN: His "baby sister" liked the idea. (*To* TIM) She says the Beekman Arms is— "so cute", Tim.

RICHARD: (*Continues*) Marian, I'm betting that Andrew first met Gilliband there—in Albany... They both pretty much grew up there...

(BARBARA *returns with a tray of glasses, silverware and napkins.*)

RICHARD: Now Gillibrand and Albany, that's really... (*Same gesture with the fingers*) They're like...

MARIAN: Are they?

RICHARD: Big time.

BARBARA: (*To* MARIAN) That can't still be warm.

MARIAN: I think it's fine, Barbara. (*The plates*) I'll take these upstairs.

BARBARA: Tell them both that they can join us...

MARIAN: I'll tell them... His Mom's not going to want to...

BARBARA: *(To* JANE*)* I put the salad in the refrigerator. *(To* RICHARD*)* What are you talking about?

MARIAN: "Albany."' *(She goes with the plates.)*

BARBARA: She makes it sound like it's Sodom and Gommorah.

RICHARD: *(Smiles)* Not far from the truth. I tell my friends, Tim, I have jumped into the muck, I just hope I can float. *(Smiles)*

BENJAMIN: What does that mean?

BARBARA: I don't know Benjamin. *(To* RICHARD*)* So why live there?

RICHARD: I work there. *(Then continues to* TIM:*)* Gillibrand. Her grandmother... Big time Albany. I never really "got" Gillibrand—the idea, the concept of "Gillibrand" —but then you go to Albany. I really get it now.

BARBARA: I'm glad... *(To* BENJAMIN*)* Do you know who Gillibrand is, Uncle?

BENJAMIN: No.

RICHARD: That's my point—people don't know who the hell she really is.

TIM: I should come up to Albany and let you show me around.

RICHARD: You should. Everybody should. *(Looks to* BARBARA, *then:)* Jane had a good time, didn't you?

JANE: I did.

RICHARD: You weren't bored.

BARBARA: I've been to Albany. *(To* JANE*)* The mall. *(Fixing up the casseroles, etc)* So you had a good time with Richard, Jane? In Albany?

JANE: I did.

RICHARD: *(Over this)* Jane…

JANE: What??

RICHARD: Tell them about that statue in the museum. It's a good story.

JANE: It's not really a story—

RICHARD: Tell them.

JANE: More of an—observation… *(To* BARBARA*)* I was in the Albany museum— *(To* TIM*)* Doing my research. I was not slacking off. I think Tuesday? And there's a medieval statue there of a naked girl. Upstairs, right as you go in. She is looking down at her hand, holding something. I just stared at her for the longest time. There was something so familiar about her. I couldn't figure out what.

BARBARA: Did she look like someone—?

JANE: No. No. Then I realized: she was in the exact pose of someone scrolling through their iPhone. *(Then)* Same look. Exact same look.

*(*JANE *puts down her plate and demonstrates.* RICHARD *laughs, shows* BENJAMIN *how the statue was standing.)*

JANE: But she was holding a cross.

BENJAMIN: I don't understand.

JANE: *(Over this)* It was just an observation…

RICHARD: I'm not sure one week in Albany is really enough—

JANE: It's enough.

*(*BARBARA *laughs.)*

JANE: We'll do it as a buffet, don't you think? And just sit where we want…

BARBARA: *(To* RICHARD *and* TIM*)* Gentlemen, come and serve yourselves.

(The men move to the table.)

BARBARA: I'll get you yours, Benjamin.

(They begin to serve themselves:)

RICHARD: *(To say something)* How's the "inn", Uncle? I hadn't asked.

BENJAMIN: I don't know. Fine. *(To BARBARA)* Isn't it?

TIM: *(Another thought)* Benjamin's in a singing group now.

RICHARD: Really? Uncle, I'm not surprised.

BENJAMIN: Am I?

RICHARD: *(Over this, to JANE)* They were just singing-

TIM: *(Over this)* "Gentlemen singing." That's on the schedule. He and four other "gentlemen", they perform once a month. We all go down to see him…

RICHARD: Do you…

BARBARA: *(To RICHARD)* You should come too, Richard… A minister visited Benjamin last week when I was there.

JANE: *(To RICHARD)* You won't believe this.

BARBARA: She, the minister is a she—spoke to him—*(To BENJAMIN)* like you were five years old. Didn't she?

BENJAMIN: Did she?

RICHARD: That's terrible.

BARBARA: *(Over this)* She said—'you know what song *I* love to sing?' I don't think you said anything, did you?

(No response)

BARBARA: Sometimes he remembers. Just when you think he's not going to… *(Continues)* So the minister says, "I love to sing—" and she starts singing to *Benjamin,* this very accomplished, respected artist, to this man here—she begins singing, *(Sings in a high voice)* "It's a small world after all..."

(Others groan, oh god, no!)

(Laughter)

BARBARA: What you have to put up with—just getting old. Right, Benjamin.

BENJAMIN: Right. I have to put up with a lot.

BARBARA: See what we all have to look forward to.

(And that quiets everyone down.)

(Pause as they serve themselves.)

TIM: The fries look good. A little cold...

BARBARA: Look at what Heidi wrote on them.

RICHARD: *(Reads a label)* "Look Adam—'Freedom Fries'."

JANE: He liked that... I could tell.

BARBARA: Could you really?

JANE: It's something he would like. *(Then: The obvious)* He'll hate Bush to his last breath...

RICHARD: *(To JANE)* I could tell them the coconut story.

TIM: What's that?

JANE: Another Albany—

RICHARD: Should I?

JANE: I don't know, Richard.

RICHARD: *(As he continues to serve himself)* Mario Cuomo, the dad, he tells a funny story about a man named—Dan O'Connell—O'Connell was the behind-the-scenes political boss of bosses of Albany for years and years. In Mario Cuomo's story, Dan and another guy get marooned—on a desert island.

BARBARA: *(To JANE)* Is this true?

JANE: It's a story, Barbara.

RICHARD: And there is only one coconut. Dan suggests—

BARBARA: On the whole island? *(To Benjamin, giving him his plate)* I'll get you more if you want more…

RICHARD: One. They take a vote on who should eat the one coconut. The other guy says, but that doesn't make sense—

BARBARA: That's what I was going to say.

RICHARD: *(Over this)*—we'll only each vote for ourselves.

BARBARA: Right.

RICHARD: *(Continues)* No, no let's try, let's vote, says Dan. So—they vote and when the vote is counted, Dan has won—110 to 1.

(They politely laugh.)

BARBARA: Albany sounds like a really interesting place…

(They are sitting down now:)

BARBARA: How long have you lived in Albany now? I forget.

RICHARD: No you haven't. *(He pours drinks for everyone.)*

BARBARA: And it's how far away? *(Then:)* Not that far…

RICHARD: *(To* TIM*)* The Albany Mayor for Life? That's what they called him. Corning. He's dead now. He kept in a closet in his office—glass containers—

JANE: Richard, please. He told me this.

RICHARD: You're right. I'll tell you, Tim, later.

JANE: *(Over this)* We're eating.

BARBARA: What? Now I'm curious.

JANE: You don't want to—

BARBARA: Tell us, Richard. If it is *so* interesting. I want to know all about 'life in Albany.' We should know more. It's our capital...

(Hesitates, then:)

RICHARD: Glass containers filled with preserving liquid—and in each one was a different...

TIM: What?

BARBARA: What???

RICHARD: A different animal's—penis. *(Then:)* I'm told, the Mayor would bring these penises out when he wanted to make a point to someone... To convince them to—I suppose, be on his side.

(No one knows what to say.)

RICHARD: Like trophies... Andrew likes to tell that story... *(To* TIM, *as if this explains everything)* Albany...

(Short pause)

*(*MARIAN *returns.)*

MARIAN: Nadine was fine with chicken... The mother eats anything.

BARBARA: I made you a plate...

(They begin to eat.)

MARIAN: Thank you. *(Sitting)* What did I miss?

(Lights fade.)

A Shared History

(A short time later; BARBARA *is standing, the others sit and eat:)*

BENJAMIN: What did I do? I don't remember.

RICHARD: I should bring you up to Albany, Uncle. No one remembers anything up there, from one day to the next.

BENJAMIN: Then I'd fit right in.

(Laughter)

JANE: You would…

TIM: You visited Barbara's class today, Benjamin.

MARIAN: Get it, Barbara. Show Richard.

BARBARA: *(Stops, to* MARIAN*)* Should I look in upstairs?

MARIAN: *(Shaking her head)* It's quiet.

*(*BARBARA *goes off.)*

MARIAN: *(Then to anyone)* Nadine says he's not in pain now… I meant to tell all of you that.

(They eat, then:)

RICHARD: I always say I want to take Barbara's class. *(To* BENJAMIN*)* Did you enjoy visiting her class, Benjamin? Was it fun?

BENJAMIN: I think so.

TIM: *(To* BENJAMIN*)* Do you know what today is?

BENJAMIN: No. What's today?

MARIAN: Jane, did you tell Richard about…?

RICHARD: About what?

MARIAN: Today—and Adam.

JANE: I forgot. You should tell him. *(To* TIM*)* You know.

*(*TIM *nods.)*

(BARBARA *enters with a pile of papers and some newspapers; she listens as she sits and organizes them.*)

MARIAN: *(Explaining)* When Adam learned he had the cancer…

BENJAMIN: What's today?

JANE: *(To* BENJAMIN, *pats his hand)* Sh-sh…

MARIAN: *(Continues)* You know he had started smoking again.

RICHARD: No.

BARBARA: After Evan died.

MARIAN: He tried to hide it—

BARBARA: *(As she goes through the papers)* He started again. Just like Peter Jennings—after 9/11…

MARIAN: He told me later…I wasn't with him then. We still weren't speaking. He asked his doctor—so how long? Oh, about a few months, the doctor said. Adam—you know Adam—says: could you be more specific, doctor? So the doctor tells him: Two months. *(Then)* Adam immediately does a quick calculation— *(To* BARBARA) it's what he told us…

(BARBARA *nods.*)

MARIAN: And said—oh he'd make it longer than that. He planned on making it well into November. At least as far as the 22nd. He wanted to be around for this. He didn't want to miss this. *(Then: proving his point)* He's made it to today…

JANE: *(Quietly to* BENJAMIN) Today's November 22nd, Uncle…

RICHARD: What do you think he was afraid of missing? Today doesn't seem to be about anything…

BARBARA: *(Shuffling through the papers, about the papers)* I asked them at the beginning of the week to talk to their parents—or grandparents—it's been that long—

RICHARD: Your students?

BARBARA: *(Nodding)* It doesn't seem that long ago— and see what today means to them. And then I asked them—'what does today mean to you?' If anything. If nothing, come back with that. Which—is what most did come back with. That surprised me. I guess it shouldn't. *(Smiles)* One senior she said—she's very smart, she said for her it was a 'mythological time'— 'when heroes died.'

TIM: *(Smiles)* I like that…

RICHARD: Fifty years ago is now "a mythological time"—??

BARBARA: Another said—his grandmother—she is always worrying, still—and especially, he said, during the last election—about an *Obama* assassination. Because of the tensions…? He didn't say why. His Grandma just told him there was a "Kennedy aura thing" surrounding Obama.

JANE: Is that still true?

RICHARD: "Hope and change…"

MARIAN: Richard…

TIM: *(To RICHARD)* "If you like your health insurance plan, you can—"

MARIAN: They're fixing that, Tim.

RICHARD: I think Obama's dilemma is he wants to look in the mirror in the morning and see someone who is still good. But for a politician isn't that useless, even corrosive? He's going to end up a very bitter man. You sort of see that already happening…

JANE: *(To* MARIAN*)* Billy doesn't have health insurance. His job is quote unquote part-time.

MARIAN: So is he trying to sign up—?

RICHARD: "Trying." That is the operative word.

JANE: *(Over this)* He says he's healthy. Why the hell should he pay for sick old people?

MARIAN: Because he's going to be a sick old person one day.

JANE: Oh I'll tell him *that*, Marian. *That* will convince him. He says, they've taken his whole generation and are just screwing with them.

(Then:)

BARBARA: Should I...?

TIM: Jane and I were in the city a few weeks ago. Down on east 4th. To see a friend's show. We got out of the subway and there were all these young people sitting on the sidewalk.

JANE: I told you this, Richard. *(To* BARBARA *and* MARIAN*)* They were filthy. Hands just caked in dirt. And they all had dogs with them. And backpacks. Like some lost society. *(To* TIM*)* That's what you said. *(To the others)* What are we losing? What have we given up on?

MARIAN: De Blasio's going to try and fix that. Isn't he? At least in the city. Isn't he?

(No response)

BARBARA: *(Continues:)* Anyway, one student brought up the sex...Marilyn Monroe. It was all over the map...

MARIAN: Barbara told me, that her point was to try and make it—present. For the kids.

BARBARA: That's why… *(Hands a scrap book clipping to* BENJAMIN*)* Benjamin. They love it when Benjamin comes to class.

BENJAMIN: Do they? Who?

BARBARA: My students…

JANE: You're an actor.

BENJAMIN: I am. I'm an actor.

BARBARA: Do you have your glasses?

JANE: They've seen him in movies on T V.

BARBARA: Anyway, Benjamin gets their attention.

TIM: I'll bet.

BARBARA: *(Pointing out)* There. Remember, only what's marked. Like you did today.

BENJAMIN: From here?

BARBARA: Yes. Right there.

BENJAMIN: *(Reads)* "Dallas. Nov. 22nd. President John Fitzgerald Kennedy was shot and killed by an assassin today." *(He looks up.)*

BARBARA: Not today, Benjamin. A long time ago.

TIM: *(To* BENJAMIN*)* Fifty years ago…

BARBARA: Tom Wicker. Remember him? It's such simple prose. Little details, strung together—it's like a poem.

BENJAMIN: *(Reads)* "Vice President Lyndon Baines Johnson, who was riding in the third car behind Mr. Kennedy's, was sworn in as the 36th President of the United States 99 minutes after Mr. Kennedy's death."

BARBARA: You can see the writer—as he grasps for facts—like someone drowning grabbing at the floating wreckage of his ship. He's trying to make it real— "99

minutes" in this case—in order to try and make sense
of something. Real for us or real for him?

BENJAMIN: *(Reads)* "Mr Johnson is 55 years old; Mr
Kennedy was 46."

BARBARA: The "is" and the "was". I am always so taken
aback when I see that he was only 46. My kids didn't
understand at all.

JANE: No, no.

MARIAN: How could they?

BENJAMIN: *(Reads)* "Mrs. Kennedy looked steadily at
the floor. She still wore the raspberry-colored

suit in which she had greeted welcoming crowds. But
she had taken off the matching pillbox hat she wore
earlier in the day."

BARBARA: Some kids laughed at that. The mentioning
of a "pillbox hat". Absurdity is as much a part of death
and tragedy, as it is a part of life…

JANE: Did they understand that?

BARBARA: *(Obviously)* No.

BENJAMIN: *(Continues)* "The ceremony, delayed about
five minutes for Mrs Kennedy's arrival, took place in
the private Presidential cabin in the rear of the plane.
No accurate listing of those present could be obtained.
Mrs Kennedy stood at the left of Mr Johnson, her eyes
and face showing signs of weeping that had apparently
shaken her since she left the hospital not long before."

BARBARA: "Apparently shaken." "Apparently."
That's—the very first speculation the writer has made.

JANE: He just snuck it in.

(BARBARA nods.)

BENJAMIN: *(Reads)* "As Judge Hughes read the brief
oath, her eyes, too, were red from weeping."

BARBARA: There's a comma before and after the "too." So—not just "her eyes too." But "her eyes— *(Then)* too." It's a small thing. But I wonder if that was a subtle way, maybe I'm wrong, a subtle way of the writer's to emphasize that all were weeping. Maybe even Mr. Wicker. "Her eyes—too."

TIM: *(To* JANE*)* That's interesting.

JANE: I don't think you're wrong, Barbara. *(To* TIM*)* He is a poet.

BENJAMIN: *(Continues)* "'I do solemnly swear that I will perform the duties of the President of the United States to the best of my ability and defend, protect and preserve the Constitution of the United States.' Those 34 words made Lyndon Baines Johnson, one-time farmboy and schoolteacher, the President."

TIM: "Thirty four words."

BENJAMIN: "At 2:46, seven minutes after he had become President, 106 minutes after Mr Kennedy had become the fourth American President to succumb to an assassin's wounds, the white and red jet took off for Washington."

BARBARA: The utter simplicity. We're reading *King Lear* now. It's the same with Shakespeare—there are times when language gets stripped down to almost nothing. *(Then)* When Lear says about the dead Cordelia: "no, no, no, no". *(Then)* One more thing…

BENJAMIN: *(Reads)* "The doctors said it was impossible to determine immediately whether the wounds had been caused by *on* bullet or two."

BARBARA: Right. That's just how it's written. It's a typo.

*(*BENJAMIN *hands her back the clipping and she begins to hand it around.)*

BARBARA: *The Times* back then, it prided itself on not making typos. They were actually very rare back then. So even this shows... Doesn't it? Even the proofreaders were struggling. Even a typo tells a story. "On bullet or two..."

(They look at the 'typo', then: pause.)

TIM: What else did you show them, Barbara?

BARBARA: I showed them this, Tim. *(She hands out the things she's collected; other newspapers, period magazines, etc.)*

JANE: *(Opening up a big Dallas newspaper with the headline, reads:)* "PRESIDENT DEAD, CONNALLY SHOT."

RICHARD: Where'd you get this—?

BARBARA: Tim—

TIM: When I visited my father in the summer. I had some time in Dallas. I'd always wanted to go to that museum there. They sell those. It's a reprint... But of the whole paper. And that's what is really interesting. The ads and everything...

BARBARA: The kids loved that, Tim.

JANE: *(Seeing an ad)* "$2.99 comfort bra."

BARBARA: They liked that.

(Laughter)

TIM: *(To JANE)* Show Benjamin.

JANE: *(As she shows BENJAMIN)* "Pre-Christmas sale." That's right, it was before Christmas.

TIM: Like now.

JANE: Right.

BARBARA: *(Standing)* Who wants more of something?

RICHARD: *(Engrossed in the stuff)* We can serve ourselves, Barbara. Sit down.

(As they look through the newspapers, etc:)

BARBARA: I also asked my kids—this was their assignment for earlier in the week, besides just talking to their parents. I said, could you somehow try and connect the Kennedy's to us. To yourselves. To our county, Dutchess. To Rhinebeck.

TIM: One kid—

JANE: How do you know?

TIM: They had Karen and me over to dinner the other night. I told you this. *(Continues)* One kid said, well Bill Clinton went to Gigi's during Chelsea's wedding weekend.

(Laughter)

TIM: The connection was that they were both presidents —

RICHARD: *(To* BARBARA*)* Did that count?

BARBARA: *(Shrugs)* My favorite was that same senior I mentioned; she learned that one of John Kennedy's sisters, Rosemary...

RICHARD: The one who had the lobotomy.

BARBARA: After the lobotomy—this was in the forties— guess where she was sent? Where the home was? Guess. Guess. *(Then:)* She lived there for years. Beacon. Beacon, Uncle. *(To everyone, amazed)* Beacon...

BENJAMIN: Why is that—?

JANE: Your "inn" is in Beacon, Uncle.

TIM: Called Craig House. The building's still there. Zelda Fitzgerald also was put there.

BARBARA: And Jackie Kennedy went to Vassar. Five or six of them got that. They liked knowing that.

MARIAN: Robert Kennedy Jr runs River Keeper.

BARBARA: Someone had that too. Tim, you found one—

TIM: It may not count. It's not about Kennedy, but it's about a presidential assassination and—Rhinebeck.

BARBARA: *(To* TIM*)* I told them about this this morning. They were really fascinated. I could tell. They all know the Rhinecliff station.

TIM: *(His story)* April, 1865.

RICHARD: So you mean Lincoln—

TIM: The train station in Rhinecliff—Amtrak wasn't there yet—

MARIAN: Oh the good ol' days.

BARBARA: So the trains still ran on time!

(Laughter)

TIM: It's all draped in flags and the black of mourning. Men, women, children stand on both sides of the track. It's night. Moon on the water. They hold torches. And the funeral train is heading north to— *(Looks at* RICHARD*)* Albany where the body will lie in state for a while in the Capital. But the train, instead of just chugging through, mysteriously stops. In Rhinecliff.

*(*BENJAMIN *Is now listening.)*

TIM: According to legend, a William Carroll, from Rhinebeck, is summoned to the train. Carroll is the Rhinebeck mortician. As soon as he arrives he is led up onto the flagged-draped train; the steam engine moaning as it just sits there, waiting; and he's taken into a small candle-lit room, where—there lies the body of the President. The hole in the President's head— made by the assassin's bullet—has opened. Perhaps maybe the movement of the train, maybe some other reason—but it has opened and it needs to be sewn up. *(Then)* About twenty minutes later, Carroll,

Rhinebeck's own William Carroll, black bag in tow, is
helped back down onto the station platform, mission
accomplished. He refuses any money and remains just
standing there, as the train now again on its way, fades
slowly into the night, while everyone, including now
William Carroll, waves goodbye to the President...
(Then) A little Rhinebeck history, Benjamin.

JANE: *(To* RICHARD*)* Tim has become consumed—

TIM: If I'm going to live here.

JANE: What about me?

TIM: If *we* are, then... We should know about where we
live. All that's here...

RICHARD: You mean Rhinebeck.

JANE: *(To* TIM*)* I'm not criticizing. I think it's good. He
still worries that he's going to be trapped...

BARBARA: *(To* TIM*)* It takes time...

(They eat.)

BARBARA: You're not eating, Benjamin.

BENJAMIN: I'm not hungry.

TIM: *(Changing back to the Kennedy subject)* I started
reading a book about Kennedy's Dad? The Dad had
already had his stroke, when Kennedy was killed.
When they told him—and obviously, Barbara what you
said made me think of this. About the Shakespeare.
(Then:) When the father was told about his son, the
only words he could say, because of the stroke, were—
"no, no, no, no..."

(Lights fade.)

Speech Acts

(*A short time later.* BARBARA *has opened a small journal that she brought in earlier with the newspapers and papers.*)

(BENJAMIN *is in the middle of reading. The others eat.*)

BENJAMIN: (*Reads*) "An older actor tells me that the spells in *Macbeth* by the witches are based upon real magic. And therefore you conjure evil every night, as actors we conjure whatever it is we're supposed to conjure—and that was this actor's explanation why most productions of *Macbeth* have accidents." We conjure…

TIM: I've never heard that explanation…

BENJAMIN: We conjure…

(*As* BENJAMIN *turns pages in the journal:*)

BARBARA: I thought you would be interested in this, Tim.

TIM: I am.

RICHARD: How did you get—?

MARIAN: She just said —

JANE: (*For the second time*) When Barbara visited Chicago last month—

RICHARD: I know Barbara visited—. But who—?

BARBARA: Uncle Fred's wife had it. She had it with Mom's old stuff. When I was looking for Mom's scrapbook for the Kennedy things, I found that. Benjamin must have been visiting them at some time and left it there in Chicago.

MARIAN: Most of it's about theater.

BARBARA: I think it's *all* about theater.

RICHARD: (*To* JANE) I remembered about Barbara's trip to Chicago.

MARIAN: *(To* BENJAMIN, *about the notebook)* I'm sure you don't remember that notebook.

BENJAMIN: *(Looking through the notebook)* How do you know?

(The others smile.)

BARBARA: *(To* BENJAMIN*)* Does it look familiar?

BENJAMIN: The handwriting…

BARBARA: Besides that. *(Then)* Years ago, I remember you saying you wanted to write a book about the theater, Uncle. I think that's what… Your notes. *(To the others)* His notes. For his theater book.

BENJAMIN: *(Reading)* "It should be the most unnatural place to be. Talking as if in a normal voice so perhaps a big audience can hear or feel or see or whatever. You're doing it again and again night after night. You're doing it at a funny time of night, when most people are going home or are home. There's nothing normal or natural about it, you'd think. But it can be the place where you feel most at home."

JANE: *(To* TIM*)* You've said things like that…

BENJAMIN: *(Another page, reads)* "Barbara tells me a story about how she'd run backstage…

BARBARA: When I was a kid.

BENJAMIN: "…in the hope that if she got to me fast enough in my dressing room she'd find—the character I'd just been playing. But no matter how fast she'd run she never got there in time. But she never found *me* either at first."

BARBARA: I think Mom told me I once even cried.

BENJAMIN: "The person there wasn't yet 'Uncle Benjamin' and it wasn't still the character either, something halfway in between, she said." 'Halfway.'

BARBARA: I think I just wanted you to pay more attention to me. *(Takes his arm)* I still do… *(Smiles, he smiles.)*

JANE: You are so handsome, Uncle.

(BENJAMIN just gets up.)

BENJAMIN: Can I read this outside?

BARBARA: It's stopped raining, Marian.

MARIAN: You want a cigarette?

BENJAMIN: I want a cigarette.

BARBARA: He wants a cigarette. Stay in the back yard.

(BENJAMIN goes.)

BARBARA: He has packs hidden all around the kitchen…

TIM: How does he remember where they're hidden?

JANE: You remember what you want to remember.

MARIAN: They're not really "hidden".

BARBARA: "He was something halfway in between." He must feel like that all the time…

MARIAN: Richard, Barbara found a photograph stuck in that notebook. Mom and Benjamin in swim suits. Some place with palm trees. Uncle keeps it at his Inn…

BARBARA: *(To RICHARD)* You haven't seen Uncle for a while, Richard.

RICHARD: He seems okay.

BARBARA: Does he? Marian thought it was the medicine. The 'inn' makes him take all this medicine.

MARIAN: But then we found all these pills stuffed between the cushions of our couch. He comes home every weekend, and stuffs his pills into the couch….

BARBARA: So it's not the medicine…

RICHARD: Is that safe to just…?

(Then)

JANE: *(To the others)* Tim and this teacher at Bard— *(To RICHARD)* Tim's teaching a class there. *(To TIM)* You're not just a waiter.

TIM: Just a workshop. Voice. For a few weeks.

RICHARD: *(To JANE)* You told me. *(To TIM)* She's very proud.

BARBARA: There's nothing wrong with being a waiter.

JANE: *(Over this)* And they've been talking, Tim and this teacher—

TIM: We know each other from Boston—

JANE: *(Over this)*—about writing a book together—or an essay? For a theater magazine. *(To TIM)* It sort of relates to what Benjamin was reading to us. His—notes. *(To BARBARA)* He's still having auditions all the time.

RICHARD: *(To TIM)* What's the essay…?

TIM: Comes from a British philosopher. Our idea. We're going to write it together. He's a good writer.

JANE: So are you—

TIM: This philosopher developed a theory—of what he called "speech acts"? Those moments in life when by saying something we are also doing something.

MARIAN: What does that mean?

JANE: Tell them. Explain it. It's interesting.

TIM: When I say, "I promise", I'm in fact—making a promise. *Doing* a promise. Speaking becomes then also an *act*. A speech act. In a marriage ceremony, for example, the saying of "I do", —given the right circumstances—means you're now married.

JANE: And Tim's always felt that that somehow relates to theater. Speech acts.

TIM: Maybe it's nothing. I'm not sure how to explain it exactly.

JANE: *(To* TIM *over the end of this)* Tim's friend, the teacher, thinks it could make an interesting article or book. *(Then)* It could be good. *(Then)* You get it published, and your name gets exposed in this magazine. Theater people read it—it helps, gets you noticed. Helps your acting.

TIM: That's not why—

JANE: That's what you said. *(To the others)* Tim is so worried that he's going to be forgotten, here in Rhinebeck.

TIM: You've told them that.

MARIAN: John was telling me...

(This has gotten their interest.)

MARIAN: ...this was *when* we were still seeing each other—

RICHARD: Maybe now... After...

MARIAN: Adam's not dead *yet*, Richard.

RICHARD: I didn't mean—

BARBARA: *(Explaining to* RICHARD*)* John's moved on.

MARIAN: I knew he would. Why shouldn't he? *(Shrugs)*

BARBARA: John and Marian are no longer together.

MARIAN: *(To* BARBARA*)* I saw them in the C V S, she was just staring at him. *(Shrugs)* He told me about a famous painter—he was painting a portrait. A nude. And one day, he is painting her breasts, his model's breasts, and he suddenly has the feeling—that they are empty. The model's chest is empty. Then two days later, she commits suicide. That was interesting. "Art—

(To TIM*)* whatever sort of art" —, John said, "maybe it shows us things that otherwise we can't see with our own eyes." *(To* BARBARA, *explaining)* He [Tim] was talking about art *doing* things...

(Then:)

JANE: Growing up around Uncle—around an actor, it was always difficult for me to know what was true and what wasn't true.

BARBARA: Was that just because he was an actor?

(Laughter)

JANE: Maybe. But still all the 'acting.' Was I the only one who felt this way?

MARIAN: *(Over this, to* BARBARA*)* We've talked about this too...

*(*BARBARA *nods.)*

JANE: Benjamin being an actor—how strange or odd was that for us? Richard?

RICHARD: I have never thought about it.

JANE: Didn't you ever wonder—what's acting and what's real? I think there are times when the acting can be more real—more emotionally raw and real...

BARBARA: *(A joke)* Tim's an actor too.

(Laughter)

TIM: I'm never real. *(He laughs.)*

JANE: He has an actress friend— *(Turns to* TIM*)* Kathy... Old girlfriend.

TIM: That was a long—

MARIAN: The one whose couch you slept on in Chicago?

JANE: Another one. *(She "rolls her eyes".)*

TIM: You told them about—?

JANE: *(To* MARIAN*)* You don't forget anything.

RICHARD: *(Helping him out)* I'm listening.

JANE: She had the part of Shakespeare's Rosalind. You know that play—?

TIM: They know it—

RICHARD: Do we?

JANE: Tell them. This is funny. Even if it's a bit— chauvinistic.

RICHARD: Now I'm interested.

TIM: Rosalind literally runs the Forest of Arden. She has complete control. Doing this, doing that. Incredibly organized. And my friend, she was, shall we say, not the most organized "person"—

JANE: He means "woman". Just say it.

TIM: "Female" —on this planet. But she suddenly— at home, during the run of the play—became super organized and efficient—in her private life, in her home life.
Washes everything. Cleans the floors. No more dishes piled up in the sink. Her husband— *(Turns to* JANE*)* She's been married now for like…I don't know. *(Continues)* Her husband says to her after the run of the play is over, and their apartment's a mess again— he says, in a hopeful, even desperate voice: "Kath, couldn't you play a few more parts like Rosalind?"

(Laughter)

MARIAN: Are we making too much noise?

BARBARA: Adam can't hear—

MARIAN: I meant his Mother—hearing us… Laughing.

(Then:)

BARBARA: *(To* TIM*)* Benjamin can put that in his book about the theater.

MARIAN: *(To* TIM*)* Or like a prayer…

RICHARD: What? What is?

MARIAN: Tim's—what did you call it? Speech what?

TIM: Speech acts.

MARIAN: Prayer. Praying. To speak a prayer is an act of faith, isn't it? It's *doing* your faith. By speaking…

TIM: I think he even talks about prayer too. The philosopher. In a way like that…

(No one knows what to say, then:)

TIM: I have another one for Benjamin's book.

BARBARA: What is that?

*(*MARIAN *looks toward the living room.)*

BARBARA: She can't hear, Marian. They're on the other side of the house.

JANE: *(To* TIM*)* Go ahead.

TIM: The great playwright—Beckett?

(They know who he is.)

TIM: A friend of a friend of mine was actually doing one of Beckett's plays and Beckett himself is directing him. This is obviously years and years ago. In Europe. The play's a monologue, and he has to talk into a tape recorder and shuffle around this little room. In slippers. *(Then)* Each day the designer brings in another pair of slippers for him to try. And each day Beckett says, no, no, not right! This goes on and on, days pass. They've tried twenty pairs of different slippers. Until finally the completely exasperated Beckett leaves rehearsal, goes to his nearby apartment, and comes back with—a pair of old beaten up bedroom slippers. The actor puts them on. They sort of fit. He shuffles around. Beckett "listens". And Beckett then says, "Now that's what I was looking for".

BARBARA: They were *his* slippers.

(TIM *nods.*)

MARIAN: So he wanted just to hear his own footsteps on the stage?

TIM: I suppose to him what he'd written was—personal...

MARIAN: But how would the audience know they were *his* slippers?

TIM: Maybe it didn't matter to him. Maybe, he thought, they would just somehow know that it was—true.

(*Lights fade.*)

By the Wayside

(*A short time later.* JANE *reads from a small notebook.*)

JANE: (*Reads*) "The travelers should have a note-book always at hand..." I wrote this down to give to Benjamin. Richard's idea.

BARBARA: Do you always keep that—? [notebook]

JANE: A notebook? I do. I'm a writer, Barbara.

MARIAN: (*Getting up*) I think I heard something... (*She stands to listen.*)

(*They all listen. then:*)

BARBARA: (*As a joke*) Marian, I'll bet she writes down what we say... (*No reaction, suddenly*) You don't, do you?

JANE: Barbara...

BARBARA: (*To* MARIAN) I was just joking.

JANE: Actually, sometimes I do.

RICHARD: Keep reading. This is interesting.

MARIAN: *(To JANE)* What is that from?

JANE: *How to Observe Morals and Manners.* Written in 1838. I came across it in Albany during my research.

MARIAN: I thought you were done with manners.

JANE: I'm not "done with—". I just happened across this.

BARBARA: *(About the manners)* You said if they're not going to publish your book—

JANE: *(Over this)* We thought Benjamin might be interested, Barbara… To put it in his journal. As inspiration to keep writing in his journal.

(MARIAN goes off to check upstairs.)

BARBARA: *(After her)* I didn't hear anything, Marian…

(Then:)

RICHARD: *(To JANE)* Read…

JANE: *(Continues to read)* "In all the countries of the world, groups of people by the wayside are the most eloquent pictures. The traveler who lets himself be whirled past them, unobservant or unrecording, loses more than any devices of inquiry at his inn can repair… Groups and scenes—because they reveal the thoughts of men—" *(Adds, to herself)* —and women— *(Continues)* "should be as earnestly observed and should be noted on the instant." *(Then: closing the notebook)* *How to Observe Morals and Manners.* 1838…

RICHARD: I'm so glad Uncle's still keeping his journal. Good for him.

JANE: Good for Barbara.

BARBARA: He forgets sometimes…

RICHARD: I should start doing that. Keeping a journal…

BARBARA: Are there things, Richard, you feel you need to work out? With a journal?

RICHARD: To remember things, Barbara.

(JANE *has been thumbing through her notebook, she comes upon another entry:*)

JANE: I wrote something else down. In Albany I saw a small show at the museum—the history of the book *1001 Nights*? Very fascinating. I didn't know anything... Richard thinks they're trying to reach out to the Arab community—

RICHARD: It's the state museum...

BARBARA: Is there a big Arab community— *(In Albany)*?

RICHARD: For the whole state. And there is—in the whole state. Albany is our capital. We seem to forget that.

BARBARA: Do we? I think sometimes we'd like to.

RICHARD: There are interesting things to do in Albany. Ask Jane—

JANE: You wouldn't even go with me—

RICHARD: I have a job—

JANE: *(To* BARBARA*)* He never really goes out anywhere—

RICHARD: That is so not true—

JANE: You told me you'd never been to the state museum. He just shuts himself away in his little apartment. *(Then back to the notebook:)* Anyway, you know the story—Scheherazade, she has to keep telling stories to keep from being killed.

TIM: By her husband. He's already killed—

RICHARD: I don't shut myself away...

BARBARA: *(To* JANE*)* I know the story.

JANE: *(As she looks in her notebook)* There was a quote on the wall, from some famous author. This is what I wrote down: *(Reads)* "Every Writer—is Scheherazade."

BARBARA: Why...?

JANE: Telling stories—to keep from dying.

*(*MARIAN *returns.)*

MARIAN: We've told Nadine that she can go. We can look after Adam tonight.

BARBARA: Are you sure—? Is she all right with—?

MARIAN: His mother's wishes. *(Then:)* Nadine understood. She even said to me, that's not uncommon on nights like these. For the family... *(Then:)* She hasn't yet figured out we're not his family. His mother's going to stretch out on the cot. It's fine.

BARBARA: And what could you say?

MARIAN: And what could I say. Nadine's getting her stuff together. Her car's on the street; I'll take her through the front. *(Starts to go)*

BARBARA: *(Getting up)* Should we say goodbye—?

MARIAN: *(Stopping her)* She's exhausted. And she'll come back tomorrow... *(She goes off.)*

RICHARD: Where does Nadine live?

TIM: *(Shrugs)* Poughkeepsie? Newburgh?

JANE: *(To* BARBARA*)* You think that's the right thing to do?

BARBARA: She's not a real nurse, she's an aide, so... If it's what his mother wants... *(Then)* You started to tell us about your book. The reason for spending all week in Albany...

JANE: It's not really a book. It's at best a... *(Shrugs)*

TIM: You always say that.

JANE: *(Ignoring this, continues)* I spoke to the
Chronogram about it.

TIM: *(To* RICHARD*)* Local thing. Very arty. Very 'new'
Rhinebeck.

RICHARD: Is that good?

JANE: I didn't find out as much as I had hoped to. They
had some good books, things on microfilm. I started
out—just diving into the Hudson River Painters. But
then I came across—

TIM: What?

JANE: *(Over this)* And this was what I ended up mostly
researching. I don't know why they had this stuff
in Albany. Anyway—you obviously all know the
painting—*George Washington Crossing the Delaware.*

TIM: Sure.

(They obviously do. They eat.)

JANE: So—who painted this iconic American painting?

*(*RICHARD *almost says something.)*

JANE: I know you know. I told you. They don't know.
Leutze.

TIM: *(Joking: "of course")* Leutze!

JANE: You don't know! Emanuel Leutze. A German,
not an American, a German. Who at the age of
nine, came to America, his parents fleeing political
persecution in Germany. He had some early success as
a painter. But the moment he had money in his pocket,
he hurried back to Dusseldorf, and carrying on his
parents' political beliefs, he sides with those radicals
who are hoping to create a united Germany.

TIM: When—?

JANE: Middle of 19th century. And he began looking
for a topic that would inspire—Germans.

Something to symbolize the turning tide of some revolution. And he stumbles upon: General Washington crossing the Delaware River... *(She eats.)* So in his Dusseldorf studio, in the middle of Germany, he procures authentic American costumes. And I suppose for authenticity's sake—he decides, in fact insists, on only *real* Americans posing for the guys in the boat, and for General Washington. He starts sending friends out onto the streets of Dusseldorf to find every real American they can get their hands on. Any American. They're just dragging them off the streets. Then—once in his studio, he plies them with liquor and god knows what else. So soon he's got a studio full of drunken Americans—on vacation... And then—he paints. And that is what he painted. That's what generations of Americans have found so deeply American and "patriotic". *(Eats)*

RICHARD: *(Eating)* That's what school teachers have dragged thousands of school kids to see...

JANE: My question is—what I'm asking in this essay, whenever I get around to it—is: is that something we really want to know? I mean, do I really want to look at that painting and think—they were drunk? They're having a good time in Dusseldorf and they're sauced? *(Then)* Sometimes—and I was about to say this when we were talking about the Kennedys and your class, Barbara. I wonder if sometimes—and Tim, you have kept saying this as this anniversary approached—if sometimes it's best *not* to see... Not to pick up the rock and look underneath... *(Short pause. Eating)* An essay about that.

(Then:)

BARBARA: If Marian were here, I know what she'd say.

JANE: What?

BARBARA: *That*—should be on N P R.

(They all laugh—that is so true.)

BARBARA: We were arguing about something the other day. I don't remember what. A recipe. A book. And she just held her hand like a traffic cop and said, "Stop it, Barbara, I heard it on N P R".

(Laughter)

BARBARA: "It must be true!"

(MARIAN returns.)

MARIAN: What?

BARBARA: We're laughing at you.

MARIAN: What's new? *(Then:)* Nadine gave him a kiss on his cheek. *(Then:)* He's still not responding… She'll call in the morning, and come if we need her.

BARBARA: I thought you said—

MARIAN: *If* we need her. *(She sits.)* So what about me were you laughing at?

RICHARD: That list is long. Where to begin?

BARBARA: N P R…

MARIAN: Why is that funny? Why does she think that's so funny? If it's on N P R… They know what they're doing… *(Stops herself; then)* She said again, that noise he's making—it's common. And Nadine thinks, he won't make it through the night. I said we know that…

(No one knows what to do or say.)

(Lights fade.)

Rhinebeck

(A short time later. They hardly eat anymore.)

JANE: I called Billy last night and told him about Adam. I keep thinking he'll react like a kid, but he's a grownup. *(To* MARIAN*)* He sent his love to you. Unprompted.

MARIAN: And mine back.

JANE: He wanted to know if he should come—

MARIAN: No, no—

BARBARA: *(Same time)* He doesn't have to—

JANE: *(Over this)* I told him that… And that you two were divorced and… So—he's not going to come.

MARIAN: Good.

JANE: Not even to the funeral. *(Then:)* Are you really sure that's okay?

*(*MARIAN *nods.)*

JANE: Billy asked if his dad were dying, would you all come. Because *we're* divorced. *(She eats.)* I told him of course you'd come. That that's different. *(Then: to* MARIAN*)* Maybe, he said, you and John will come down and see him some time this winter. There's some show at the museum…

MARIAN: I liked going to Philadelphia.

JANE: I didn't tell him about you and John…

TIM: *(To* JANE*)* Billy okay?

JANE: We talked for a while. I don't know how we got started—except of course Adam—. Billy said a friend of his died. Someone from Haverford. And he said there's no easy way to destroy your Facebook page. No way to just update— "Jane is dead". You just sit frozen in time until Facebook can somehow verify with a death certificate, a notarized letter from the parents, something like that—that you're dead. So his friend's page is still up, and someone somehow has gained access to it and is posting photos and videos via her name. Billy said, it is as if she is still living online.

TIM: Someone dies you want to do something. That's human. This is just human.

(Then:)

MARIAN: You're very quiet, Richard. So unlike you.

RICHARD: Is it?

BARBARA: I'm sorry it's such a trial hanging around with your sisters…

RICHARD: I never said—

MARIAN: We'll let you go soon…

(Then:)

TIM: *(To say something)* I was surprised that Adam chose Dapson's and not Burnett and White. They're right around the corner.

BARBARA: Dapson's is just—

TIM: And wasn't Adam good friends with the Burnett and White people—?

BARBARA: It's complicated. Adam's business has landscaped Dapson's for… *(To MARIAN)* He couldn't decide, could he? He didn't want to hurt either. I don't know how we ended up choosing funeral homes. I think it usually just happens…

JANE: *(About the funeral homes)* Tim's now interested in all the Rhinebeck gossip.

TIM: That's not gossip.

JANE: *(To RICHARD)* He's even thinking of joining the volunteer fire department.

RICHARD: You told me. *(To* TIM*)* That's—ambitious.

TIM: I'm almost too old.

RICHARD: I've seen guys sitting outside the station who—

TIM: To start. To take on.

JANE: *(Over the end of this)* We live so close to the station Tim told them he can just put the siren on his head and run there… *(She smiles, to* TIM*)* They didn't find that funny, did they?

RICHARD: *(Trying to say something, to* TIM*)* I've always thought that the Beekman Arms must be a nice place to work.

TIM: *(Shrugs)* It's a restaurant.

BARBARA: Years ago they used to make the waiters wear costumes. Like from colonial times? I just remembered this. I had a friend—. He worked the bar—he had a funny three-cornered hat. He really hated wearing that hat.

TIM: They don't do that anymore.

BARBARA: *(To* MARIAN*)* Tim waited on Adam's mother and the "baby sister" at breakfast today.

JANE: You didn't tell me—

TIM: I've hardly seen you.

BARBARA: They didn't know who he was. They've met a lot of people over the past two days.

TIM: I didn't say who I was. I just waited on them.

*(*BARBARA *notices* RICHARD *checking his watch.)*

BARBARA: *(To* MARIAN*)* He's checking his watch.

RICHARD: It *is* late, Barbara.

(Phone rings in the kitchen.)

*(*MARIAN *jumps.)*

BARBARA: *(To* MARIAN*)* I unplugged the phone upstairs.

MARIAN: It's probably the "baby sister"... She was worried about the noise on Route 9... *(Mimics:)* "Oh how am I going to sleep?" *(As she goes out)* I don't know what the hell she thinks I can do about it... *(She is gone.)*

BARBARA: The sister's upset. She wanted to stay too, but the Mom...

(The phone has stopped ringing in the kitchen.)

TIM: Best to stay out of that.

BARBARA: Should we make some coffee?

(No response.)

*(*MARIAN *returns.)*

MARIAN: *(To* RICHARD*)* It's Pamela...

*(*RICHARD *gets up.)*

MARIAN: She sends her condolences—to all of us.

RICHARD: *(As he goes, as a "joke")* She's tracked me down. *(He is gone.)*

BARBARA: Jane? Tell us how Albany was. How's he doing?

*(*MARIAN *sits to listen.)*

JANE: He works. *(Shrugs)*

BARBARA: What's his apartment like?

JANE: Small. Tiny. But very clean.

MARIAN: Really?

TIM: Why is that—?

BARBARA: Does he have a cleaning lady?

JANE: No.

BARBARA: *(To* MARIAN*)* Good for him.

JANE: I was there the whole week. He did the dishes. The grocery shopping.

MARIAN: Does he cook?

JANE: He tries. He got a book. And he follows the directions. I wouldn't have believed that, if I hadn't seen it. He doesn't just make it up.

TIM: Why is that—?

BARBARA: Does he have any friends there?

JANE: I don't think so. I didn't meet any.

(BARBARA *and* MARIAN *share a look.*)

JANE: *(Again:)* He works. And spends almost nothing. There's nothing on the walls. Not even a calendar. Like a monk.

MARIAN: Why is he punishing himself? He didn't do anything.

JANE: He's so angry.

BARBARA: *(To* MARIAN*)* He tries to hide it.

JANE: He keeps telling himself: Pamela is going to want more money. "Nothing is ever enough." His words. "She'll never be satisfied. She never is." He told me he "thinks" she's going to sue him... Once he gets started on that, he doesn't stop.

(Sisters share a look.)

BARBARA: Sh-sh...

(They listen.)

BARBARA: I thought he was coming. *(Concerned)* I don't hear him talking...

JANE: Tim, would you stand there and warn us if he's coming?

TIM: No.

JANE: He spoke to Pamela last night.

MARIAN: To Pamela? He called her?

BARBARA: *(To* MARIAN*)* Pamela told me this morning.

JANE: *(To* BARBARA*)* After you called about Adam getting worse. To tell her he had to come here. It's Richard's weekend with the kids. He said they fought.

BARBARA: *(To* MARIAN*)* She said—he just yelled at her. *(Getting up)* I don't hear him... *(Listens)* Is he off the phone? I'm going to go see. *(She goes into the kitchen.)*

MARIAN: *(Sighs)* Jesus... *(She looks off toward the living room.)*

JANE: Adam seems quiet, Marian...

MARIAN: *(Getting up)* I'm going upstairs. I'll be right back. *(She goes.)*

*(*JANE *is alone with* TIM.*)*

JANE: *(Sighs)* What a night... Thank you for staying. I know you don't want to.

TIM: It's fine. I'm family. Aren't I?

*(*JANE *smiles at him.)*

JANE: Now I want a drink...

(As TIM *goes and pours:)*

JANE: You know you are a wonderful actor, Tim. And you *should* still audition... Even from here. The train's just...

TIM: I know...

(Then:)

JANE: And Karen's going to get over this—whatever she's going through. I was like this too at her age. It's a good place for kids.

BARBARA: *(Returning)* Richard's out in the yard with Benjamin. They're—smoking cigarettes together.

JANE: Richard hasn't smoked since college...

(As BARBARA *looks around:)*

JANE: She went upstairs. *(To* TIM*)* You don't smoke. You'd better not.

TIM: No, I don't. I don't.

*(*BARBARA *looks around the room.)*

BARBARA: A woman who used to live here...

TIM: This is interesting.

BARBARA: She just appeared at the back door last Sunday. She said she'd lived here, in this house, first as a child, then, to take care of her mother. Her mother, she said, died here—in this very room. *(Then)* They'd brought down a bed. They'd brought down a bed from upstairs. It was pretty much where this table is...

JANE: We thought of doing that for Adam... *(Then:)* *(About the dinner)* I think we're done.

*(*RICHARD *returns.)*

RICHARD: Uncle's out in the yard, looking—lost. I should go. Where's Marian?

BARBARA: Don't go yet.

RICHARD: Barbara—

JANE: Marian's upstairs. She's coming right back.

(As they wait for MARIAN*:)*

JANE: *(To* RICHARD*)* Are you smoking?

BARBARA: *(To* RICHARD*)* How's Pamela?

RICHARD: I'll live. My cross: Pamela...

JANE: *(To say something)* Barbara had a guest this week, someone who used to live in this house.

RICHARD: Did they just knock on the door?

*(*BARBARA *nods.)*

RICHARD: I've done that. Our house on the South Side. Years ago. They wouldn't let me in.

BARBARA: She said that when they had the chimney removed—you know how you can still see the base of it in the basement? They found a bill from a store. Dated 1863. She said she'd send it to me. That it belonged here.

RICHARD: A bill for what?

BARBARA: She didn't say. And here... Here... *(She points to a place on the floor.)* I'll show you... *(She gets on her hands and knees and pulls back a corner of the rug.)* Here, look here. I covered this with the rug on purpose. She showed this to me. Over here.... Look, she said, see these little cuts? See?

(Others go and look.)

BARBARA: They were made, she said, by one of her sons, showing off his new hunting knife.
The knife slipped and the boy cut his foot and had to go to the hospital. The father gave him hell, she said.

(MARIAN enters seeing BARBARA on her knees and others around her. MARIAN has a small baby monitor.)

TIM: Barbara's visitor...

(MARIAN nods.)

RICHARD: *(Getting off his knees)* How long was she—?

BARBARA: Not long. Marian was out. I wanted her to meet her. *(To MARIAN)* Things okay?

(MARIAN holds up the monitor.)

BARBARA: *(About the monitor)* Good idea.

MARIAN: *(Explaining to BARBARA)* I thought—. His Mother falling asleep...

(MARIAN turns it on—a little static and the ticking of a clock upstairs.)

RICHARD: *(In a whisper to* MARIAN*)* I was just waiting for you to come back down.

MARIAN: *(Smiles)* They can't hear you, we can only hear them.

RICHARD: I wasn't. I've had children…

MARIAN: He thinks they can hear us.

BARBARA: I was telling Richard about the woman who visited…

MARIAN: Did you tell him that they'd brought a bed down here? For the Mother?

BARBARA: I told him. *(To* RICHARD*)* Sit, sit.

MARIAN: So she died, right here… We think pretty much where the table is—

RICHARD: She said.

MARIAN: She left. I never did meet her… We almost did that for Adam…

BARBARA: Such an interesting way of looking at your own house. Through—her eyes… For her everything was just different. Everything changed. *(Then:)* Who wants more to eat? Richard? Salad?

RICHARD: I'm done.

(On the monitor: "Marian, thank Barbara for the dinner"*).*

MARIAN: "Thank Barbara for the dinner." His Mother.

*(*MARIAN *turns the monitor down.)*

MARIAN: She didn't thank me…

BARBARA: This is a mess.

JANE: *(Getting up)* I'll take some things in. And get the trays.

RICHARD: *(Standing)* I should go now.

BARBARA: Sit, Richard. Just for a few more minutes. Please. And visit with Marian. She's hardly even seen you…

(RICHARD *hesitates and looks at his watch.*)

BARBARA: Don't look at your watch.

(RICHARD *sits.*)

(JANE *picks up a few things and goes off.*)

MARIAN: *(To* RICHARD*)* I sat with Adam one night a few weeks ago and we talked about all that had changed in this village. He was already here… He wasn't going back to his apartment. *(To* BARBARA*)* He never should have sold our house. *(Then)* Barbara was so generous…

BARBARA: You live here too. It's your house too. You were generous too.

MARIAN: *(Continues)* We—in our imaginations because he couldn't even be moved by then—we "walked" down Market Street; first one side, then the other. And we told each other—what we remembered being there.

TIM: What do you mean? Jane might write a history of Rhinebeck.

MARIAN: There have been at least two already—

BARBARA: She always has so many ideas—

TIM: She just has to write one, Barbara.

MARIAN: *(Answering* TIM's *earlier question)* What's no longer there or changed, Tim. The C V S—that *was* the grocery store. The A & P.

(JANE *returns with trays; and the sisters begin to pick up.*)

MARIAN: The honey store was the hardware store…. Moving the statue of that sexy soldier from the fire station to the parking lot. *(Then)* Adam remembered the day a house, a whole hundred-and-fifty year-old house on Mill Street, *(To* RICHARD*)* Route 9, they lifted it up, put it on wheels and rolled it down about a block and a half—. That's where it is now.

BARBARA: *(To* TIM*)* Part of the Beekman's expansion. That house in the back.

MARIAN: *(Continues)* There was the pizza church. Adam remembers it being a sort of hippy art center in the sixties—that's even before me... He did a performance there once—against the war... With a bunch of people he was living with at Rokeby.

JANE: I can't imagine Adam as a hippie.

MARIAN: *(Smiles)* I'll show you pictures. As long as I can cover up me. Tim, Adam reminded me—do you know what Mill Street, Route 9, becomes if you go south far enough? It becomes —Broadway. *The* Broadway in Manhattan. Route 9, our Mill Street...

TIM: *(Sort of a joke)* So I guess I'm not *that* far from Broadway.

*(*JANE *smiles and pats* TIM.*)*

MARIAN: Barbara said, her visitor was very happy that schoolteachers were living in her house. And not goddamn rich lawyers from New York City who crowd everything out on weekends.

*(*MARIAN *has looked at* RICHARD.*)*

RICHARD: I live in Albany.

JANE: Tim told me the other day—

TIM: What?

JANE: *(Over this)* Above the pizza place? He heard this at Bard. The woman who heads the trust for the composer—John Cage? Do you know who that is?

RICHARD: I don't.

JANE: *(Over this)* Well she—the head of the trust—lives in Rhinebeck above the pizza place. I don't know why, but that seems so fascinating...

(Then)

RICHARD: Benjamin and I noticed that they've been building some sort of stage—behind your house, Barbara.

BARBARA: The back of the town parking lot.

TIM: For Sinterklaas...

BARBARA: *(Over this)* The parade.

JANE: Tim's been working on this year's. With Karen. They're making stars.

BARBARA: *(To* RICHARD*)* They do a little show on that stage, Richard. Saint George and the Dragon... *(To* MARIAN*)* Adam was Saint George once or twice, wasn't he?

MARIAN: Two years in a row. *(To* TIM*)* Evan and I did stars. For about three years, until we just had fights. I'm sure you're having a better time.

JANE: *(To* MARIAN*)* Karen and Tim have fights. *(Turns to* TIM*)* I can tell them that. We live here.

BARBARA: *(To* MARIAN*)* You had some very good times together. You two. Come on.

(Short pause; they listen to the ticking.)

(No one knows what to say.)

BARBARA: *(Reaches and takes* MARIAN's *hand)* This woman, Richard—you should know this about your sister—what she has been doing for her ex-husband. These past few months. I can't even begin to describe... *(Then:)* She stopped everything to take care of Adam. Gave up everything...

RICHARD: I know.

MARIAN: What did I give up?

BARBARA: She pretty much moved back in with him into his apartment. How much do you know?

RICHARD: I think we're all proud of Marian for all she's done.

BARBARA: How much do you know? You haven't been here-

RICHARD: Jane's told me.

MARIAN: His apartment was—not a place to die in. *(To* BARBARA*)* That's what you said. *(Then)* I've learned I can do the 'bedside thing.' I hadn't thought before I could. Could I have a drink? Not that I'm going to feel it.

*(*TIM *goes to pour her a drink. A small yawn on the monitor.)*

MARIAN: The mother—yawning. *(Continues)* It finally dawned on me—must really be dying from a broken heart. Evan, she broke his heart. When she killed herself. She broke my heart. *(Looks up at* BARBARA*)*

BARBARA: We're family. It's just us. You're safe…

MARIAN: *(Smiles, then)* For some reason, it hasn't killed me yet. I sometimes wonder why. *(Then)* Just three months ago—I don't think I could even have imagined spending five minutes with Adam. He'd hurt me so much. But, at Barbara's urging—

BARBARA: You didn't need me.

MARIAN: *(Over this)* Her insistence—we all know what that can be like…

BARBARA: *(A joke)* What does she mean?

(Laughter, maybe too much laughter)

BARBARA: Hey, hey…

MARIAN: What would we do without Barbara? We heard about Adam being sick; and she took me literally by the hand to visit him. And so I saw so clearly… what I just said. Once I saw that, and saw that him blaming me—*that* I could now forgive—because it is so obvious that he blames himself so much more. And in the past month, I've come to see that he is the last person on earth I have left to share—to share Evan with.

(Before BARBARA *can say anything:)*

MARIAN: I know, you too. But…it's different. So doing the bedside thing was easy. Even selfish. *(She suddenly gets up.)* I should do some dishes.

JANE: They can wait.

BARBARA: She wants to do dishes…

*(*MARIAN *starts to head off and stops.)*

(Then:)

MARIAN: *(Trying not to cry)* Adam and I sat up one night a few weeks ago. "Sat up." He couldn't sleep anyway. He was on his drugs. And together we counted up how many places in Rhinebeck Village there now were where you can eat. When we moved here, there were three. We counted—and came up with twenty-eight. Now there's twenty-eight places to eat here… *(She goes and picks up the monitor and heads into the kitchen with it.)*

*(*BENJAMIN *passes* MARIAN, *as he enters:)*

BENJAMIN: Why is Marian crying?

BARBARA: She's losing Adam, Uncle. They'd been married for thirty years.

BENJAMIN: That's a long time. I'm sorry.

BARBARA: The grass must still be wet. Are your shoes wet?

BENJAMIN: A little.

BARBARA: Did you get cold outside?

BENJAMIN: I did get cold.

BARBARA: Please wear your coat.

RICHARD: I'm sorry it's been so hard on her. I hadn't completely…

BARBARA: No. You hadn't…

JANE: *(Noticing* BENJAMIN *watching)* You know Adam, Uncle?

TIM: *(To* BENJAMIN*)* You and I talked a lot about Adam today.

BENJAMIN: Adam's upstairs. He's dying.

JANE: That's right. *(To* TIM*)* That is right.

RICHARD: I should head back.

BARBARA: Do you have to?

RICHARD: *(Standing up, ignoring her)* Benjamin, always good to see you.

BARBARA: You know who he is, Benjamin?

BENJAMIN: Richard.

RICHARD: *(To* BARBARA, *making a point)* He knows who I am. *(To* BENJAMIN*)* I'm so glad you're safe at that 'inn.' I'm so happy all that worked out… For everyone. And now maybe Barbara's getting out more too… And doing things for herself… *(Turns to* JANE*)* Jane, thank you for visiting me in Albany. I had a really nice time with you. Tim… Thank you for loaning her out. *(Turns to* BARBARA*)* I'll say goodbye to Marian in the kitchen. Barbara… *(He goes to kiss her goodbye.)*

BARBARA: Can we talk for a minute, Richard?

RICHARD: About what? I have to go…

BARBARA: About that. About going.

RICHARD: Barbara—

JANE: Tim…

TIM: Benjamin, I'm going to check out that stage in the parking lot. You want to come?

BENJAMIN: No.

TIM: I'll take some of these into the kitchen.

(*As* TIM *heads off with a tray:*)

RICHARD: *(To* TIM*)* What do you know that I don't know?

JANE: Maybe he just wants to have a smoke, Richard.

RICHARD: Tim's smoking?

JANE: No. *He* isn't.

RICHARD: *(Then)* Barbara, what do you want?

BARBARA: How are the kids? Still angry at you?

RICHARD: I'm trying to buy them off. Tickets to shows, ballgames. I'm trying…

BARBARA: It takes time. So I'm told. Kids… So Samantha's the toughest on you?

(RICHARD *nods.*)

(MARIAN *returns with monitor.*)

BARBARA: I guess girls usually are with their fathers. And Baby Mike is…okay?

RICHARD: I guess. And he's not a baby, Barbara. He's now a teenager.

BARBARA: Sorry, an Aunt thing.

MARIAN: We all do it.

JANE: We do.

BARBARA: I've never said it to his face.

MARIAN: No…

RICHARD: Don't. Please…

BARBARA: Are you all right, Richard?

(RICHARD *looks at her and his sisters.*)

BARBARA: Maybe this isn't the right time to ask. Tonight. But when have we had the chance to ask? We haven't seen you in months. I call—and we talk for a couple of minutes—and then you're busy, or you have another call—. Or you're outside and your hands are cold.

RICHARD: I'm busy. I have a new job.

BARBARA: Why have you been avoiding us?

RICHARD: I just spent a whole week with Jane. Jane?

(No response)

RICHARD: What is this? *(Then)* I'll try and call more often. You're not going to make me feel guilty, Barbara. You've done that enough for one night. So just stop.

MARIAN: Richard, we're worried about you in this "Albany".

RICHARD: Is that what you're worried about? Jane? You just visited me. Tell them. I'm fine. Tell your sisters I'm fine.

(No response)

RICHARD: *(Smiles)* "Albany"? , Marian, trust me, I know what I've gotten myself into. My eyes are wide open. I'm ready to be terribly disappointed by Andrew Cuomo. We all better be prepared for that. *(Smiles)* I'll be fine. I'm fine. I appreciate the concern. Thanks for the talk… *(Stands)* Now my dear sisters I really need to go.

JANE: *(Stopping him)* Richard…

MARIAN: You're hurt. And you're just doing what you've always done, Richard, when you get hurt.

RICHARD: Which is—?

BARBARA: You run away. And you hide… *(Then:)* And bury yourself in something…

MARIAN: We're worried, Richard that you've buried yourself in Albany.

RICHARD: I have a job. I'm trying to do something good. What am I supposed to do? What do you want me to do?

BARBARA: We'd like you to move here.

RICHARD: You're joking. *(He smiles.)*

MARIAN: No…

BARBARA: Go and work there. Try and do some good. Maybe you can. Who knows? And it's less than an hour away. So then every night, come home here… Please don't smile. We hate that smile. What?

RICHARD: *(Smiling)* Pamela warned me—probably the only true thing she ever said to me—the only *honest* thing—your sisters, she said, will never be happy, Richard, until you're living in fucking Rhinebeck. Well, I guess she was right. Unbelievable.

BARBARA: Pamela's worried about you too.

RICHARD: What? What are you talking about—?

MARIAN: She's called us. Calls us.

JANE: A lot.

(Then)

RICHARD: You can't understand.

BARBARA: Try us, Richard. We want to understand.

RICHARD: The three of you have done nothing but criticize her since the day you met, and now—

MARIAN: And now we're not defending her, except to say she's not the monster, Richard, that you need her to be.

BARBARA: Marian—

RICHARD: Jane?

JANE: I agree with them, Richard.

BARBARA: But Pamela's sorry. And she's worried about you too… Like us. Your sisters…

MARIAN: She's not going to "sue" like you told Jane. And you know that, Richard.

RICHARD: *(Over this)* What?

BARBARA: *(Over this)* She's not trying to keep you from the kids. And you know that too. She knows she's hurt you. And she's very sorry, Richard.

RICHARD: *(Over the end of this)* If Pamela could hear this… She must have said to me a hundred times— watch out, Richard, your sisters don't have lives of their own up there in Rhinebeck, and once Benjamin…

(JANE looks at BENJAMIN.)

RICHARD: They're not going to rest until they find someone else's life to run.

MARIAN: Meaning yours?

BARBARA: *(Same time)* I don't think that's true.

RICHARD: "I don't know why can't they just live their own fucking lives."

BARBARA: We have lives.

RICHARD: The three of you have done nothing but make fun of her.

JANE: That is not true.

RICHARD: *(Over this)* Nothing she has ever done has been good enough. You think she didn't know that?

You think that didn't hurt her? That didn't hurt me? I
guess it's no wonder she left me...

JANE: *(Over this)* No. No, Richard.

BARBARA: *(Same time)* No. Richard... Pamela left you—
because she fell in love with someone else. *(Short pause)*
And we're sorry... *(Then:)* Please, think about what
we've said. But now, stay the night. It's late. You're
upset. You shouldn't be driving back upset.

JANE: How about a drink, if you're not driving now...?
You've been making yourself drink seltzer all night.

(Then:)

BARBARA: If you want, until you find something better,
you could stay here. There's a full bath downstairs.
Even has its own entrance. It's blocked now, but we
can open it up. I can move into Benjamin's room.

BENJAMIN: My room...?

MARIAN: Only when you're not here, Benjamin. And
Jane and Tim are just down the street...

(Short pause)

JANE: Everyone ready for dessert?

*(On the baby monitor there is a static noise of the monitor
being picked up, and a woman's voice whispering:
"Marian...")*

MARIAN: I thought this might be a mistake. She always
tried to get me to wait on her... *(And she goes out into
the living room and upstairs.)*

JANE: You having dessert, Richard?

(RICHARD doesn't say anything.)

JANE: *(To BARBARA)* Richard never says no to ice cream.

BARBARA: The church ladies brought pies.

JANE: What church ladies?

BARBARA: At Marian's church.

JANE: That's who those ladies were… Any ice cream?
Richard likes ice cream.

BARBARA: I don't know. Marian buys the ice cream.

JANE: Let's look.

BARBARA: I know Marian has chocolate sauce…

(BARBARA *and* JANE *go to the kitchen.*)

(*Then*)

BENJAMIN: It will be all right, son. That's what I always
try and tell myself…

(*Lights fade.*)

Evan's Baby Monitor

(*The same.* BENJAMIN *and* RICHARD; TIM *has just entered:*)

TIM: The rumor is—you're staying for dessert. Good.
(*Then*) Adam told me a story about meeting a girl at
the bar at Foster's years ago. That's your old hangout
Benjamin.

BENJAMIN: Is it?

TIM: This is when Adam could still tell stories. And this
girl at Foster's is an actress. She's just graduated from
acting school. And she's in Rhinebeck because she has
just gotten her first professional acting job.

RICHARD: In Rhinebeck?

TIM: That's what Adam said he asked. I think he meant
this as a cautionary tale…

RICHARD: Where in Rhinebeck? And this was years
ago? That pizza church that Marian was—?

TIM: No, no—the Aerodrome. You okay?

(RICHARD *shrugs.*)

TIM: Adam said at that time he'd never been to the
'famous' Aerodrome—it wasn't a very cool thing to do
and it cost money. And you could see the planes fly
over the village for free, so… But the girl was cute, and
he was curious…

RICHARD: *(Back to the story)* This was before he'd met
Marian…

TIM: Before they'd… *(The story)* So one Saturday
morning Adam goes to the Aerodrome to watch this
cute girl do her first show; he sits in the bleachers in
front of a big open field. *(Continues)* Two World War
I planes—those bi-planes—the evil Red Baron's and
the other's, the hero's, they are in a quote unquote
"dogfight" overhead. *(Then)* The owner comes out of a
tent, with his megaphone and with the young actress
now in a short white skirt, on his arm and he leads her
to a stake in the middle of the field, and ties her up
there. And the crowd goes wild.

RICHARD: You're kidding.

(JANE returns with the bowls for ice cream, etc.)

TIM: And through his megaphone the owner explains
that this is Truly Truegood, the hero's girlfriend, who
has been captured by the evil Red Baron. She looks up.
And the Red Baron—being evil I suppose—wants to
harm her. The owner runs off the field. And the dog
fight continues above, but now the Red Baron from his
plane, begins to—little white sacks, and they sort of
explode when they hit ground. Bombs. Aiming at this
tied up young girl.

(RICHARD shakes his head.)

TIM: She squirms—I suppose that was her acting.
And she shouts things that are drowned out by the
airplanes' engines. Those were her lines. And all the
time the Red Baron's bombs—they get closer, closer to

the young wiggling innocent actress… *(Then)* Adam, then just looked at me, smiling, and said: "Maybe there's a job out at the old Aerodrome that's right for you. Rhinebeck, Tim."

(BARBARA *returns with ice cream, chocolate sauce, etc.*)

JANE: I think he was just trying to scare, Tim—being an actor. He was trying to mess with you.

BARBARA: He *could* be mean. Adam. Really mean. Ask Marian.

(MARIAN *enters, she holds a book.*)

MARIAN: Yes he could. *(As she turns on the monitor)* I told the Mother to lie in my bed, in my room. She's exhausted. I said we had the monitor. I'd wake her…

(The ice cream is served.)

BARBARA: *(Ignoring this)* And his Mother agreed?

MARIAN: Not at first.

BARBARA: *(Serving)* Was she crying?

(MARIAN *nods.*)

BARBARA: It can just sneak up on you… Of course it can.

MARIAN: She said—for someone who couldn't help Evan, I've been real nice to her son… *(Handing the book back to* BARBARA*)* She said she didn't like this.

(They take that in, then:)

BARBARA: She's tired… Marian, there's chocolate sauce.

(MARIAN *takes the chocolate sauce.*)

BARBARA: *(About the book)* Did she even look at it?

MARIAN: I don't know.

TIM: *(Reads the title)* Jane Austen's Letters.

MARIAN: It's Barbara's.

RICHARD: *(Over this)* Who writes letters anymore?

JANE: Who's going to know how we lived? I've read that. [the book] Beautiful thoughts about very trivial things. What will be left for others to know about *our* everyday life?

MARIAN: *(To* TIM*)* You want to borrow it?

*(*TIM *shakes his head.)*

MARIAN: *(To* JANE, *about* TIM *and the book)* Too girlie for him.

*(*BENJAMIN *stands.)*

BARBARA: You don't want your ice cream, Benjamin?

BENJAMIN: I'm not hungry…

BARBARA: What are you going to do?

BENJAMIN: Lie down…

BARBARA: He wants to lie down.

BENJAMIN: I just said that. Why do you repeat everything I say? I'm tired. *(He goes.)*

BARBARA: He's tired. *(To* MARIAN*)* He didn't take a nap…

RICHARD: He seems older…Benjamin.

MARIAN: "Benjamin."

JANE: *(Watching where* BENJAMIN *just left, musing)* Are you my father, "Benjamin"?

(Short pause)

RICHARD: *(To* JANE*)* We could just find out. It's easy enough now to find out. We've all talked about this. Do we want to know now?

(As they eat:)

JANE: *(Picking up the Jane Austen)* I love reading people's letters. The "little things" in life. I'm thinking of pitching something like that as a book.

BARBARA: *(Eating)* Jane always has so many ideas.

JANE: *(Continues)* Family Bibles, keepsakes, journals... Like that bill discovered in your chimney, Barbara. Small things that might have meanings larger than... Than you think they would.

MARIAN: She'd seen a ghost...

JANE: What??

MARIAN: Adam's mom. That's what she was crying about, she said. A ghost hovering over Adam in his bed. *(Then:)* A girl... *(Then: about the baby monitor)* She was calling me to come and see her. To see "it".

BARBARA: Did you? Did you see— "it"?

MARIAN: No.

RICHARD: She's tired.

(As they eat:)

MARIAN: A couple of days ago. I heard that squeak the school bus makes when it stops? Probably from Market Street. And I could see Evan, with her My Little Pony backpack. The way she stood, all sassy, proud. Years and years ago? Hand on hip... *(Demonstrates)*

(BENJAMIN returns.)

JANE: Can't you sleep, Benjamin?

BENJAMIN: I'm hungry.

BARBARA: He's hungry. *(To BENJAMIN)* You're very restless, aren't you?

BENJAMIN: I feel restless.

BARBARA: He's restless.

TIM: Let's get Benjamin some ice cream. Would you like ice cream?

BENJAMIN: I would, Tim. I like ice cream.

TIM: I certainly know you do. Sit with us, Benjamin. Every time we walk into town, we have to stop at 'our' new fancy gelato place.

RICHARD: Rhinebeck has a fancy gelato place?

BENJAMIN: It's expensive isn't it?

TIM: That's what we say every time. "It's really expensive…"

BARBARA: *(To* RICHARD*)* It's not for us.

(As they eat and serve BENJAMIN*:)*

JANE: A couple of weeks ago. *(To* RICHARD*)* I don't think I told you this.

TIM: What?

JANE: You know. Barbara's embarrassed by this.

RICHARD: Now I'm interested. What? What embarrasses Barbara?

JANE: *(To* BARBARA*)* Forgetting (BENJAMIN*)*—

BARBARA: Oh that. Don't listen, Benjamin.

BENJAMIN: What?

BARBARA: Cover your ears. *(As she eats:)* A couple of weeks ago, we all go to the mall. Jane and Tim in their car. Marian and Benjamin—it's the weekend so Benjamin's here—in my car. I'm looking at H & M, they're in the music store… I think he's with them. They think he's with… We get home, take off our coats, put on the kettle—and someone says —

MARIAN: I said:

BARBARA: "Where's Benjamin?" *(She reaches and takes* BENJAMIN's *hand.)* We'd forgotten you... Do you remember that?

(BENJAMIN shakes his head.)

BARBARA: He actually enjoyed just wandering around the mall by himself. You weren't scared at all... *(Then)* You like being alone sometimes, don't you?

BENJAMIN: I do.

(As they eat:)

JANE: At the "ceremony" today in Dallas... They kept away anyone who might—

TIM: "The crackpots."

JANE: They just wanted it to be... What? I don't know. What is it? What are we supposed to be remembering?

BARBARA: We watched a bit in class today. Those poor people looked like they were freezing. I kept thinking, why couldn't it have been that cold and raining back then.

MARIAN: I don't understand.

TIM: Because they'd have had the car roof *up*, Marian.

BARBARA: That historian spoke well. I loved his book on the Brooklyn Bridge. The Navy Glee Club—that must not have been fun in that weather. The reading of the speeches... "Where power corrupts, poetry cleanses." I made my kids write that down.

JANE: I'm sure you did, Barbara.

BARBARA: The tolling of all the city's bells... The moment of silence—at the exact time he was shot.

(Pause)

JANE: Adam still gets angry when anyone calls him a 'progressive.'

BENJAMIN: Why?

JANE & MARIAN: *(As Adam)* "Because, we're fucking *liberals!* Suck it up, Apples!"

(Laughter)

BENJAMIN: Why is that funny?

MARIAN: He thinks we've given up. Or we've forgotten what we are. He thinks we're lost, Benjamin.

(Short pause)

BARBARA: One of my kids, in the middle of our discussion today—he asks me: so what do you remember, Miss Apple? About all that. That—day. *(Then)* The first thing that came to mind was— *(Smiles)* that it was only a few months later after—Kennedy's death—that the Beatles came to America and were on Ed Sullivan. I told the kids, I think our excitement—our squealing—it was our way of—releasing. We hadn't been able to do that for a while, and so it had just built up.

TIM: You hold things in, they just come out...

BARBARA: I then said something that surprised even me. I wonder if it's true. It just came out. Tell me if you think it's true. I said—I wonder if there are two kinds of fears in the world. One kind, you learn from your parents. Like spiders, and traffic or "Nazis". I certainly was scared of them.

JANE: *(As a "joke")* I still am.

BARBARA: Then there's this second kind of fear. The fear we learn on our own, from your own experience of the world. For me, the assassination was that kind of fear. Maybe the first of that kind of fear for me. For an eleven-year-old girl. I was an eleven-year-old girl, whose father had just left.

MARIAN: Father was still there later.

BARBARA: The first time. When he left that first time, Marian. You don't remember that. Only Richard and I remember that. *(Then:)* How we learn that at any moment the world can change. And there's no one to protect us. A fear like that.

(Then:)

RICHARD: *(It just comes out)* The first person I saw die— was Lee Harvey Oswald...

MARIAN: I think that's true for a lot of people our age.

TIM: The first time I saw someone die?

JANE: *(To* TIM*)* Who did you see die?

TIM: My sociology teacher in college. Collapsed in our class. They tried to... For weeks I kept "seeing" him walking around the campus. I'd see other people but think it was him. I think my brain was just trying to work things out...

JANE: That's what we do... We work things out...

MARIAN: *(The same point)* I dreamed of Adam last night.

JANE: There you go. Working things.

BARBARA: A nightmare?

MARIAN: Not really. Maybe.

BENJAMIN: I don't remember my dreams...I wish I did...

BARBARA: He doesn't remember his dreams.

RICHARD: He said that, Barbara.

TIM: *(Over the end of this)* Know where the word "nightmare" comes from?

RICHARD: Where does it come from?

TIM: The "mare" refers to demonic women; who suffocate sleepers by lying on their chests. *(Then)* My recurring nightmare—

JANE: Talk about working things out. Listen to this.

RICHARD: What?

TIM: I mean, what used to be my recurring nightmare.
It came off a movie. Years ago. A couple have a child,
a little girl—the child dies. They're devastated. They
visit Venice. He's something do with restoring art. And
there have been all these terrible murders in Venice.
No one knows who is doing them. Then the man sees a
little girl in a red cape—his daughter wore a red cape.
He follows her, along the canals to a church. She runs
up the stairs, higher and higher and he runs after. He
reaches the top, opens the door—she's not there, then
he turns and hiding behind the door is a dwarf, with
a beard, in a red cape—with a knife raised… *(Then:)*
That's what I would dream. All the time. I'd walk into
a room, no one there, then behind the door—someone
with a knife. And as it plunges into my skull, I scream
and wake up. *(Then:)* One day, I thought enough is
enough. I decided to do something about this. I found
the movie on D V D, this was still years ago, and then
even the screenplay, published. In a used bookshop. I
chose an afternoon—so it would be light. And I started
the movie and followed along in the screenplay,
stopping to read ahead, so I couldn't be surprised. And
that did it. I beat it. I stopped having the nightmares. I
healed.

RICHARD: Good for you.

JANE: He's not done.

TIM: I was so proud of myself. After I was confident
that the nightmares were gone, I told my then wife
about this. She asked if she could see the movie. Then
I couldn't find it. I couldn't find the screenplay either.
I went to a store—I think Virgin, and learned that—the
movie hadn't come out on D V D. And the screenplay
had never been published. *(Then:)* So I hadn't read and

watched it again. Not in real life. We're working all the time I think—healing ourselves. Trying to.

MARIAN: One day about four weeks ago, we'd just moved Adam here, to take care of him. I return from school, Adam I know is asleep. The aide, the one we had before Nadine, she comes downstairs, I pay her. It's a grey day. I don't turn the light on in here. I hear a voice, "Hi Mom". Come from the kitchen. 'You're back. Hi!' I heard it. And then I saw her. I saw her expression and her face, as she came out of the kitchen. And walked right past me. Right here. *(Then)* I swear to god—I could smell her. Where's...? Shit...! Shit...! *(Suddenly realizes the monitor is off, she grabs it and turns it on and off.)*

JANE: What's wrong—?

MARIAN: *(Hurrying off upstairs)* It's off.

TIM: It's...off. Probably just the batteries. Barbara where do you keep your batteries?

JANE: In the kitchen—

BARBARA: In the drawer next to the silverware—

RICHARD: Are you sure it's the—? *(He picks up the monitor.)*

TIM: *(As he hurries off into the kitchen)* I don't know...

RICHARD: *(To BARBARA)* We would have heard something. The Mother's in the room.

BARBARA: *(Shakes her head)* The other bedroom.

JANE: Should we go up...?

BARBARA: Wait. Wait...

(Then as they wait)

JANE: *(To BARBARA)* She saw Evan?

BARBARA: I've read that pretty much a majority of people who suddenly lose a loved one—especially mothers with children—they see them or smell them or feel their touch.

(TIM *returns with batteries he and* RICHARD *Put them in the monitor; the sisters and* BENJAMIN *watch as:)*

BARBARA: They think it's like how when you lose an arm or a leg, suddenly. And then you still feel it. It's the memory that is real. One feels the memory physically. It is more real than anything. There but it isn't there. I know that feeling.

(The monitor comes on; the clock is heard ticking from the bedroom.)

RICHARD: Sounds like it's okay.

JANE: Or like children and their imaginary friends who can seem totally real… There to fill a need. Something missing… I had an imaginary friend, Trousers. Remember?

*(*BARBARA *nods.)*

*(*MARIAN *returns.)*

MARIAN: Everything's fine… Thanks. The mother's back in the room. She can't sleep either.

(They listen to the monitor for a moment, then:)

BARBARA: *(To* MARIAN*)* God knows how long those batteries had been in there… *(To* JANE*)* We just started using… *(The monitor)* Marian found it in box. It'd been for Evan. When she was a baby.

RICHARD: I've been asked to be on the board of a school for the blind.

BARBARA: What? How are *your* eyes, Richard?

RICHARD: My left eye—

BARBARA: Still?

JANE: It's always going to be blurred, Barbara. He's told us that.

RICHARD: Someone in Andrew's office is involved. He thought... He thinks I'd be a good fundraiser. It's upstate. Near Utica. I visited...

BARBARA: You visited? When?

RICHARD: I don't tell my sisters everything. And I do get out. *(To* JANE*)* I didn't go out at all this week because I wanted to visit with my sister. I have friends. *(Then:)* One of the kids surprised me, she said, "you know, mister, blindness is a way of life that's not entirely unfortunate." That's a quote from a blind South American writer. They have it on a wall there, in braille. *(Then:)* She said, this kid—really smart kid, as she gave me a tour, —she said, people born blind—like herself— "We don't just hear sounds, we can hear objects. We can hear objects as we approach them. Objects at head height, they slightly affect the air currents reaching the face..." *(Then:)* We were talking about healing. But I wonder if it's not about trying to heal ourselves. But embracing how we cope. We find ways. People do. *(Then, an example:)* Congenitally blind children, I'm told, usually have superior memories...

(They look at BENJAMIN*, then:)*

BARBARA: You're so handsome. Jane was saying that earlier. I agree...

BENJAMIN: Thank you.

RICHARD: The girl said as I left: "Too often people with sight don't see anything..."

MARIAN: Nadine was telling Adam's mom and me— she's been through this. It's her job.

JANE: I couldn't do that job. Every day—

MARIAN: I see the rewards.

TIM: What was she saying—?

MARIAN: That, often when someone is very close to dying—they begin having what you could call "fantasies". Their way of coping I guess, Richard.

JANE: Remember when Mom—

RICHARD: She was delirious.

MARIAN: That's an interpretation.

BARBARA: What did Nadine say about these "fantasies"?

MARIAN: That she listens carefully to them. Sometimes even notes them down.

JANE: I'd like to see that notebook.

MARIAN: A dying person working things out. Or so she at first thought. But then she wondered if they weren't something these people needed to say, to convey to us—

TIM: To us?

MARIAN: —something they'd now seen which we haven't.

RICHARD: I don't believe that.

MARIAN: But now—she says she doesn't know. And so she just writes them down in this notebook. She said, maybe someday someone will read it and figure it out.

(Then:)

JANE: Remember when Mom lost her hearing, and she started to hear songs? Songs she said she didn't even know. What was *that*?

(BARBARA reads from a pile of papers held together with a clasp. [she brought these in earlier with the other papers.])

BARBARA: *(Reads)* "I'm good with death."

JANE: What?

MARIAN: You have that. Good. Richard should hear these. Read them.

RICHARD: What's—?

MARIAN: Her students.

(BARBARA *looks up.*)

BARBARA: *(To* MARIAN*)* Maybe he doesn't want to...

RICHARD: I don't know what they are, Barbara.

MARIAN: She asked her students—this week—about death. Write about what you think when you think about "dying".

BARBARA: Not exactly. The idea was "The Kennedys and death". I figured some of their parents would be thinking about that—this week. Today. But I said they could just write about death too. A lot did. *(Then: reads)* "I'm good with death."

RICHARD: What does that mean?

BARBARA: *(Reads)* "I'm good with death. And it's important to accept oneself in the now, in case you die at any moment, because you won't always be able to die old and have the chance to be 'at peace' with your life."

RICHARD: How old?

BARBARA: Luke's sixteen.

RICHARD: Good luck, Luke.

JANE: *(To* TIM*)* "I'm good with death."

BARBARA: *(Reads)* Another one: "Death gives meaning and structure to life." Jamie.

TIM: Sure. Why not?

BARBARA: One of the great perks of being a teacher—is that you have people who will try and answer your questions. *(Smiles, reads)* "Death is not a negative thing."

MARIAN: *(Smiling)* Speak for yourself, young person.

BARBARA: *(Reads)* "Because death forces us to take responsibility for the shape of our lives."

MARIAN: I read them to Adam. God knows what he heard.

BARBARA: *(Reads)* "Because there is death, people feel more accountable."

JANE: Do they? *(To* TIM*)* Do we?

BARBARA: "People are shaped by experiences and environments but unpredictability gives life shape."

TIM: Can I see?

(BARBARA *hands* TIM *the clasped papers.)*

BARBARA: I agree with that…

TIM: *(Reads)* "Unpredictability gives life shape…" Is he saying—

BARBARA: *(Over this)* She.

TIM: That life then has no shape? *She already* thinks that?

BARBARA: I wrote some older students that I'm still in touch with. They're mixed in.

TIM: So up to college age—?

BARBARA: And they're all mixed together. No order.

JANE: *(To* TIM*)* Read out loud.

TIM: *(Reads)* "We are all slowly, day by day, piece by piece, creating our own deaths." What does that mean?

RICHARD: She's bullshiting…

TIM: I don't know.

RICHARD: I talked like that when I was that age. I know B S.

TIM: I talked like that too. I think sometimes I still do. *(Smiles)*

JANE: I don't think it's B S. They're reaching... Don't just dismiss it. I think she is saying like that other boy: it's something we learn to live with... Part of what we are. And I agree with that.

TIM: Another. *(Reads)* "When my grandmother died, I remember hearing Mom saying to Dad, 'when anyone dies, Henry, we find ourselves asking—what we are doing with our lives. That's only natural." *(Then:)* Another one. *(Reads)* "I go into Special Collections in the library—"

BARBARA: She's in college.

TIM: "—into a vault with the oldest books. When I get down there, it feels so trippy because you completely lose yourself in this other place in the fabric of time. That person's reality that you are reading feels so alive and vibrant, so I'm skeptical about any delineation made between people who are living and people who are—then." "Then."

(JANE takes the book.)

JANE: "People who are then..." For her they're just 'then.' I love that. I love that. Why do I love that? *(Reads)* "We think very much of time being linear—"

BARBARA: I like this one. I like her.

JANE: *(Over this)* "— but recently I've been feeling like time is more like an ice rink, circling around, sometimes connecting with those from an earlier time period who have a similar path to yours, and feel similar emotions." She's a poet, this girl.

(BENJAMIN *has picked up the Jane Austen letters and is reading it.)*

JANE: Listen to this: *(Reads)* "Death—is very rarely on my mind."

(Laughter)

RICHARD: Good for her.

MARIAN: How long will that last?

JANE: *(To* BENJAMIN*)* You're reading the Jane Austen...

BENJAMIN: I am.

BARBARA: He's read it before.

MARIAN: Not too girlie?

BENJAMIN: No.

JANE: "My life is so contingent on getting shit done that I don't think about death."

(Laughter and a few "True. That's me too".)

JANE: Another: 'Death, it takes care of itself!'

(Bigger laughter)

(Church bells off, it is midnight.)

(JANE hands RICHARD the notebook, and looks at her watch.)

JANE: Adam made it, Marian. Through the whole god damn day. And why did that mean so much to him?

MARIAN: I did ask him that.

JANE: You did?

TIM: What did he say?

MARIAN: That it was one of the very few times, fifty years ago, maybe the only time in his life, when he felt our whole country was connected.

JANE: So then it wasn't the assassination—it was the coming together.

MARIAN: He said, "let's at least remember that."

TIM: *(Then)* Some state government recently –. This is what we've come to. They hired a guy to actually measure the worth of life in their state.

RICHARD: What??

TIM: To put a dollar value on a life in their state. They wanted to raise the speed limit and knew that was going to cause more deaths. But it was also going to give people more time—because they'd get to places faster. So he counted the hours saved by people getting to work earlier, at so many dollars an hour—and then divided that by the number of deaths that would increase because of people driving faster. So he came up with a dollar figure for the value—of a life in that state.

JANE: That's just stupid.

TIM: Some psychologist, for a study, began asking people how much they would need to be paid to give up something.

JANE: You told me this.

RICHARD: *(Over this)* What do you mean? Give up what?

TIM: Like how much for a good tooth. How much for your—little toe? And he got prices…

RICHARD: How much for a little toe?

TIM: I don't remember. Less than you'd think. He got prices.

MARIAN: Who were these people?

JANE: A "scientific" survey of normal people—like us.

TIM: Like a restaurant menu. Toes. Ears. Whole feet… It's one way to look at ourselves. I suppose.

RICHARD: I don't know about anyone else but I was really surprised when I heard that Adam was now going to church. Adam... Of all people...

MARIAN: I go to church. Sometimes I take Benjamin.

RICHARD: Adam always made such a point about those "religious people".

MARIAN: He meant—

RICHARD: I know what he meant. He had beliefs. I admired those beliefs. They just weren't 'religious beliefs.'

MARIAN: Richard, maybe he—

RICHARD: I don't want to talk about it.

MARIAN: What is so wrong about talking about religion?

RICHARD: I didn't say it was wrong.

MARIAN: That's what I heard.

RICHARD: As long as it's not just "Oh my god, I'm going to die. Help me."

MARIAN: Oh come on, why can't we be stupid or sentimental or scared or hypocritical—if that's what you have to call it. But if we don't talk about what we're scared of...? What scares us... No one can hear us. I'm scared.

BARBARA: There's more than just us, I think, Richard. And to answer something you implied about us a half hour or so ago, I don't think it is a waste of a life to live for other people. I don't think that diminishes one. Makes your life less valuable...

(They listen to the ticking on the monitor.)

BARBARA: Adam asked me to recite something. He wanted— *(Corrects herself)* —wants us all to do something. He told me he thought this was very fitting...

RICHARD: Is it religious?

MARIAN: Go into the kitchen if it embarrasses you.

RICHARD: I would like to hear, Barbara. *(To* MARIAN*)* I'll behave...

MARIAN: Good.

RICHARD: *(Then:)* Is it religious?

MARIAN: When will you grow up?! Richard!

JANE: Barbara, I'm listening. Go ahead.

BARBARA: It's from a Greek play. Spoken at someone's funeral. I've already memorized it. I thought I should be ready... *(Recites:)*
"First let the year of mourning begin
Let every head be shaved.
Let every garment be black.
Let the cavalry
Crop the manes and tails of the horses
Throughout the city
Let every stringed instrument be unstrung
Let every flute lie breathless.

But then, after, we must sing
In defiance of this loathsome god
Who collects our bodies
Like a debt collector."

(Then:) That's how Adam wants his service to begin...

(Lights fade.)

In Barbara's House

(The same a short time later; TIM *has a piece of paper with the instructions for Adam's funeral service.* JANE *sings [Psalm 13]:)*

JANE: *(Sings)*
How long Jehovah, wilt thou me forget for aye:
How long-while wilt thou hide thy face from me
   away?
How long shall in my soul, my counsels set dayly
Sad sorrow in my heart, how long shall my foe be
Exalted over me?

(Short pause)

TIM: *(To* RICHARD*)* Adam liked her voice. Likes. *(Reading from notes:)* Then—next for his service, Adam wants... *(Looks up to* BENJAMIN*)* Benjamin?

BENJAMIN: What?

MARIAN: Barbara?

BARBARA: *(She gets up)* If we're practicing. *(To all)* We are practicing. Is that what we're doing?

JANE: No one's going to bed.

*(*BARBARA *heads into the living room.)*

MARIAN: *(Calls after her)* I think I saw it on the top of the piano, Barbara...

JANE: *(Handing them out)* The first songs ever sung in America, Richard.

RICHARD: Tim said.

MARIAN: By white people.

TIM: I was showing Richard earlier. Then his mother is going to say something.

MARIAN: She'll talk about Evan. Evan hated her...

TIM: *(To* BENJAMIN*)* And then you're next, Benjamin.

BARBARA: *(Returning with a small book)* He wanted this. *(Corrects herself)* Damn it, *wants* this...

BENJAMIN: What is it?

BARBARA: For Adam's funeral, Benjamin. He's wants everyone to do something at his funeral. He wants you to read this.

BENJAMIN: For his funeral?

MARIAN: After he dies. Adam's dying.

TIM: We're practicing. Will you read it?

MARIAN: Adam saw you perform this at BAM, Uncle.

JANE: We all did.

BARBARA: Your Gaev... *(She hands* BENJAMIN *the book)* The bookcase speech...

*(*BENJAMIN *looks at the book.)*

BARBARA: From *The Cherry Orchard,* Uncle. A play you were in. Long ago... A different time.

BENJAMIN: Adam's still upstairs...?

*(*BARBARA *nods;* BENJAMIN *speaks toward the monitor.)*

BENJAMIN: Hello, Adam...

RICHARD: Benjamin, he can't—

MARIAN: Richard, Sh-sh.

BENJAMIN: I've read this before?

MARIAN: You have, Uncle. Many, many times. You've just forgotten...

TIM: *(To* BENJAMIN*)* Gaev is looking at an old bookcase—in a child's room. This child has died... —and the household has never recovered from this death. Adam and I talked about this. He told me— some deaths you just never get over...

(Then)

BENJAMIN: *(Reads)* "Do you know, Lyuba, how old this bookcase is?" *(Looks up)* Why is he talking to a bookcase?

BARBARA: *(Hesitates then)* Uncle, why don't you just say it to the table. Talk to the table…. It's there… *(To others)* Why not?

(BENJAMIN *looks at the table, then:)*

BENJAMIN: Then why don't I just call it a table?

(Laughter)

BARBARA: Sure, Benjamin. You can do that…

BENJAMIN: *(Reads)* "Do you know, Lybua, how old this—table is? Last week I looked underneath and read what was burnt there. This table was made exactly one hundred years ago. Now what do you think of that? Huh? We could celebrate its centennial jubilee. It may not have a soul, but I don't care what you say— it's a hardworking table." *(Looks up, smiles)* "Yes, this thing." *(Touches it)* "My dear friend and honored table! I congratulate you on your existence. Which for one hundred years has supported only the highest ideals of virtue and justice. Your silent summons to profitable labor has never wavered these hundred years. During such time you have upheld virtue, faith, hopes for a better future for a new generation of our race…"

RICHARD: What's next?

TIM: Number thirty-nine.

BARBARA: We've practiced this.

TIM: This is just the women.

BARBARA: Or—just the "girls". He always had to call us "the girls".

MARIAN: He thought it was funny. Sometimes Adam was a son of a bitch.

WOMEN: *(Sing)*
I Said I will look to my ways,
lest I sin with my tongue;
I'll keep my mouth with bit while I
the wicked am among...

BENJAMIN: *(Into the baby monitor)* That was for you
Adam. *(Then:)* Should we all tell him that...?

(They hesitate, then as they begin to speak to the monitor:)

WOMEN: "That was for you, Adam..." "Hi Adam..."
"For Adam..." etc.

RICHARD: *(To* JANE*)* It sounds religious. I think he got
religious.

JANE: Think of it as music, Richard.

TIM: Then his sister releases the ashes into Crystal
Lake...

JANE: *(To* RICHARD*)* I'll show you later... Just behind
South Street.

TIM: She is not to say anything... He even wrote that
down. *(Shows them)* "My sister is to say nothing."

BARBARA: What's next?

TIM: Twenty-three. And that's last.

RICHARD: Short and sweet.

MARIAN: It's late November, he was worried it might
be too cold. So he wanted to keep it short.

BARBARA: *(To* MARIAN*)* He could be thoughtful.

MARIAN: He could.

JANE: *(To* RICHARD*)* We all sing this.

TIM: *(To* RICHARD*)* Everyone. He's even underlined:
everyone.

*(*MARIAN *passes out music.)*

BARBARA: This is a famous one, Uncle.

MARIAN: *(To* RICHARD*)* We've been practicing. Try and follow along… Adam jumped over a lot of the "God stuff" in this one, Richard.

RICHARD: So it's not religious.

MARIAN: And here—he changed "in the Lord's House" to "in Barbara's House". Doesn't really scan. But that's what he wants. There— *(Reads)* "in Barbara's House—"

BARBARA: I told him—Barbara and Marian's house.

MARIAN: That doesn't fit, Barbara. You can't sing that.

BARBARA: That's what I told him. That's what it is.

MARIAN: *(Reads)* "And in Barbara's House I shall dwell for long as days shall be…" Ready?

ALL: *(Sing)*
Yea though in valley of death's shade
I walk none ill I'll fear,
Because thou art with me, thy rod,
And staff my comfort are.

For me a table thou hast spread
In presence of my foes;
Thou dost anoint my head with oil
My cup it over-flows…

Goodness & mercy surely shall
All my dayes follow me:
And in Barbara's house I shall dwell
For long as days shall be.

(Short pause)

TIM: That's it. That's the end…

*(And the "play" is over, a pause as first "*BARBARA*" and then the other actors look out into the audience.)*

*(And then "*BARBARA*" speaks to us.)*

"'BARBARA": *(To the audience)* And so we live. Sometimes we come together. Something brings us together. And some days we are alone. But it's those days together, that remind us, why we live. Or, maybe it is—how. How—we live…

(Lights fade.)

END OF PLAY

REGULAR SINGING (OR SINGING BY NOTE)

"The true and ancient mode of singing psalm-tunes according to the pattern of our New England psalmbooks, the Knowledge and practice of which, is greatly decayed in most congregations."
Thomas Symmes, 1720

NOTE

REGULAR SINGING is the final play in a four-play series about the Apple Family of Rhinebeck, New York, my home. Like each of the first three plays, Regular Singing was written to open on the day it is set, Friday, November 22, 2013 or the fiftieth anniversary of the assassination of President Kennedy.

When I began this series, I wrote about how I felt it was quite likely that these plays would end up "disposable", by which I meant that they are so specific to time and events that they would soon be out of date. Perhaps foolishly and with a certain amount of hubris, I have come to think or at least hope that the plays might have a somewhat longer shelf life and even, when experienced as a group over two or four days, might even add up to something greater than its parts. We can soon see. Surrounding the opening of REGULAR SINGING, the other three plays will be remounted with the same cast.

In notes for the earlier plays, I mentioned the importance of having an ensemble of actors, who come together year after year, bringing with them the sense of a real family. And I have mentioned how supported I have been by Oskar Eustis and the Public Theater, which has commissioned each of the four plays *and* announced their openings before they were written. Such confidence in a writer is very rare. And I am grateful. What I have yet to mention is that most every

Saturday night over the past many years a small group of friends has spent a few hours in my living room, talking—about life, themselves, their hopes, their art, their jobs and parents and families, what they have been reading and seeing, and, of course, about their country. The Apple Family plays originate from those Saturday nights.

In my note for **Sorry** I quoted the theater visionary Harley Granville Barker, and I do so again: "One is tempted to imagine a play—to be written in desperate defiance of Aristotle—from which *doing* would be eliminated altogether, in which nothing but *being* would be left. The task of the actor would be to interest their audience in what the characters *were*, quite apart from anything they might *do;* to set up, that is to say, the relation by which all important human intimacies exist."

And I wrote in that note that it is my hope that these plays are about the need to talk, the need to listen, the need for theatre, *and* the need to be in the same room together.

Maybe it's really just saying the same thing another way, but after completing **Regular Singing**, I want to add that I hope that these plays are about the need to talk, the need to listen, the need for theater, the need to be in the same room together *and* the need to know, in small and even some bigger ways, that we are not alone.

Finally, I end with another quote from Mr Granville Barker, a writer and thinker who has profoundly influenced my own thinking and ambitions:

"What livelier microcosm of human society...can there be than an acted play."

I read and consulted many books and articles while writing REGULAR SINGING; here are the most important: Oliver Sacks' *Hallucinations* and *An Anthropologist on Mars;* James Thomas Flexner *History of American Painting* (three volumes); David Nasaw's *The Patriarch,* Paul Grondahl's *Mayor Corning,* Robert S McElvaine's *Mario Cuomo,* William Kennedy's *O Albany,* John P Papp's *Albany's Historic Street,* Stephen Rodrick's *New Yorker* article, "The Reintrodution of Kirsten Gillibrand", William Safire's essay for *The New York Times,* "The New Rainmaker"; Sari B. Tietjen's *Rhinebeck Portrait of a Town,* Michael J Sandel's *Justice,* J L Austin's *How To Do Things With Words,* Tom Wicker's reporting for *The New York Times* on the assassination of President Kennedy; the newspaper Tim holds up is a copy of an issue of *The Dallas Times Herald*; Thomas Walter's *The Grounds and Rules of Musick Explained*; Lorraine Inserra & H Wiley Hitchock's monograph *The Music of Henry Ainsworth's Psalter*; the compact disc collection *America Sings: The Gregg Smith Singers.* The story of the actress playing Rosalind is stolen (without her knowledge) from my friend, Jemma. The story of Samuel Beckett's slippers is from my friend, Gregory. Barbara recites from Euripides' *Alcestis* as translated by Ted Hughes. My daughter Jocelyn and her friends Evan and Margaret were very helpful in describing what such an event of fifty years ago might mean to a younger generation today.

R N
Rhinebeck, 2013